BASKETBALL
Skills & Drills

SECOND EDITION

Jerry V. Krause, EdD
United States Military Academy—West Point

Don Meyer
Lyscomb University—Nashville, TN

Jerry Meyer
Vanderbilt University—Nashville, TN

Human Kinetics

Library of Congress Cataloging-in-Publication Data

Krause, Jerry, 1936-
    Basketball skills & drills / Jerry V. Krause. -- 2nd ed.
      p. cm.
    ISBN 0-7360-0171-9
    1. Basketball--Coaching.   I. Title.   II. Title: Basketball skills
  and drills.
  GV885.3.K68 1999
  796.323'.077—dc21
                                        98-52768
                                           CIP

ISBN: 0-7360-0171-9

Acquisitions Editor: Jeff Riley; **Developmental Editor:** Joanna Hatzopoulos; **Assistant Editor:** Amy Flaig; **Copyeditor:** Don Amerman; **Proofreader:** Jim Burns; **Graphic Designer:** Robert Reuther; **Graphic Artist:** Francine Hamerski; **Photo Editors:** Amy Outland and Clark Brooks; **Cover Designer:** Keith Blomberg; **Photographer (cover):** Allsport; **Photographer (interior):** Tom Roberts; **Illustrators:** Roberto Sabas, line drawings; Tom Roberts, Mac art; **Printer:** Versa Press

Human Kinetics books are available at special discounts for bulk purchase. Special editions or book excerpts can also be created to specification. For details, contact the Special Sales Manager at Human Kinetics.

Printed in the United States of America   10 9 8 7 6 5 4 3 2 1

Human Kinetics
Website: http://www.humankinetics.com/

United States: Human Kinetics, P.O. Box 5076, Champaign, IL 61825-5076
1-800-747-4457
e-mail: humank@hkusa.com

Canada: Human Kinetics, 475 Devonshire Road Unit 100, Windsor, ON N8Y 2L5
1-800-465-7301 (in Canada only)
e-mail: humank@hkcanada.com

Europe: Human Kinetics, P.O. Box IW14, Leeds LS16 6TR, United Kingdom
+44 (0) 113-278 1708
e-mail: humank@hkeurope.com

Australia: Human Kinetics, 57A Price Avenue, Lower Mitcham, South Australia 5062
(08) 82771555
e-mail: humank@hkaustralia.com

New Zealand: Human Kinetics, P.O. Box 105-231, Auckland Central
09-523-3462
e-mail: humank@hknewz.com

Contents

Preface

" I seek to leave the world a little
better place than I found it. "
—James Naismith, Inventor of Basketball

Better Basketball Basics was the original book that focused only on fundamental skills of the game. This 1981 publication became popular with coaches and sold out its two printings. In 1991, the concepts of this book were refined and developed into the first edition of *Basketball Skills & Drills.* The 1991 book quickly became a best-seller basketball teaching and learning reference. Over 50,000 players and coaches agree that this book is becoming the simplest, most comprehensive treatment of basketball basics, the fundamental skills of the sport.

Basketball Skills & Drills, Second Edition, is a significant improvement of the successful first edition. There are plans to release a CD-ROM version of this book in the near future. The addition of Don Meyer and Jerry Meyer as co-authors brings new contributions of successful playing and coaching expertise from two more generations of linked experts who have built their careers around successful execution of basketball fundamentals. We hope this "Skills and Drills" package will be a legacy for future basketball players and coaches.

This edition brings to bear over 100 years of overlapping, related basketball experience (all age and skill levels and both genders) concentrated on the basketball basics. Thus, *Basketball Skills & Drills* can function as the definitive source of fundamentals for coaches, players, and players' parents alike. It is designed to be the primary basketball reference focused on elementary/middle/secondary school and youth basketball levels. It also can be used as a fundamentals-focused textbook for basketball coaching theory classes. Improvements include

- more focus on elementary/middle/secondary school-age basketball,
- a basic and advanced section of both skills and drills,
- reference to players and coaches who also emphasize fundamental skills,
- addition of court diagrams and clear, accurate illustrations,
- identification of critical cues (keys for teaching and learning), and
- expansion of the team tactics and drills section for coaches.

The basic skills are the foundation for success at all levels of basketball. For example, Michael Jordan, maybe the best ever to play the game, combines the proper and quick execution of exceptional fundamental skills with great natural abilities. These superior skills were developed through years of dedication to continuous improvement resulting from proper and quick execution of these skills through specific, carefully developed drills.

Acknowledgments

Primary appreciation goes to the *players*—the young men and women we have been privileged to work with and learn from. The opportunity to learn from players is the catalyst for this fundamental foundation reference. It is our hope that future players will benefit from it as much as we have from developing it. Special thanks go to these players as examples to learn from:

> for Jerry Krause—to Don Meyer who was a student of the game even when he was a player.
>
> for Don Meyer—to Jerry Meyer who was not only a coach on the floor but a role model for demonstrating fundamental skills.
>
> for Jerry Meyer—to Evan Abrahams as a player.

In addition to these people, there are always mentors that are positive influences on our personal and professional growth and development. Some of our most important role models have been:

John R. Wooden, former basketball coach at UCLA who is enshrined as a player and coach in the Naismith Basketball Hall of Fame. He has always been patient and understanding in providing time and help for aspiring coaches, as well as being a model professional as a coaching educator. All of the coauthors appreciate his guiding light.

George Sage, longtime physical education teacher and coach. Sage was a highly respected head coach who Krause had the privilege to work with and Don Meyer had the good fortune to play for. His example as a true professional, educator, coach, and friend has been a steady guide for us. Jerry Meyer cites Don Meyer, Mike Roller, and Ricky Bower as three great coaches who taught him to play and coach and shaped his overall vision of the game.

Finally, a debt of gratitude is always owed to those who are a primary source of inspiration in our personal lives:

> from Jerry Krause—my friends and family, who have provided personal relationships that are the balance for my basketball world.
>
> from Don Meyer—to Bruce Hoffman, my first basketball coach; Hank Overin, my first baseball coach; Bill Foster, who taught me a work ethic; and all the coaches and players who taught me the game and, more importantly, the love of the game.
>
> A special thanks to my dad, now deceased, who showed me everyday what toughness means.
>
> from Jerry Meyer—to my wife, Mary Kate, and our child, Owen Rainer, my immediate family (mother, father, and two sisters), grandparents, and Aunt Nancy, for their support.

Basic Body Control

"Footwork and balance are necessary *every moment* of a game while ballhandling is needed less than 10 percent of the game."

—Pete Newell, Hall of Fame coach

One of your first and foremost tasks is to teach players how to move and control their bodies. Fundamental movements are sometimes called the *basics* of basketball; they are essential tools for each of your players to learn.

You will need to teach each player to move effectively (the bottom line is getting the job done) and also efficiently (moving the best way). Teach players to conserve time and space and to reduce wasted motion so they can develop balance and quickness. In other words, your players should always move with a purpose. In essence, basketball is a game of balance and quickness—all movements should focus on those purposes.

Basketball is a game of quickness (hand and foot) and speed (overall body motion), used at the proper time. Your coaching should continually emphasize the principle of doing things right, doing things quickly, and then making the right move quickly at the right time. All this should be done while developing and maintaining individual, physical, emotional, and team balance and offensive and defensive position.

The six fundamental positions and movements of basketball that you will teach are stance, starts, steps, turns, stops, and jumps.

QUICK STANCE

Critical Cue

Play and stay low to the floor. Get in and stay in a quick stance.

Your players need to learn to be ready to move at all times, developing the habit of a good basic basketball position to ready them for quick movements. Teaching quick stance is a challenging task, and you will need to be patient with younger players who may not have the strength and muscle endurance to stay in position very long. The most important part of quick stance is getting players in and keeping them in bent knee/bent elbow positions. All joints should be flexed and ready. The game is played low to the floor. The lower players get, the higher they can jump, the more explosive their moves to the basket, the quicker they are on defense, and the better they can protect the ball.

Critical Cue

Quick stance test— sit in chair with head behind knees.

Teach players the feeling of quick stance—being ready for anything, feeling quick. Maintaining basic position is hard work; players must become comfortable in an awkward, unnatural, monkey-like position. Set into the stance—get low. Remind them frequently to get in *and* stay in their stance. If you consistently emphasize quick stance early, your athletes soon will learn to assume it automatically. Quickness is a combination of thinking quick, feeling quick, and becoming quick by improving skills.

A good test for quick stance is to imagine sitting in a chair with the head positioned behind the knees, as shown in figure 1.1.

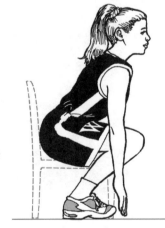

Figure 1.1 Quick stance test (side view).

Foot Position

The best foot placement in most situations is the *slightly* staggered stance, toed outward. Feet should be at least shoulder-width apart, with the instep of the front foot along the same horizontal line as the big toe of the other foot

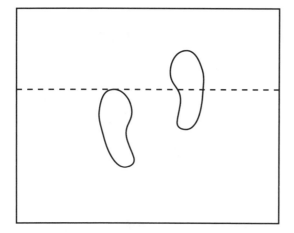

Figure 1.2 The staggered stance (top view). An instep-and-toe relationship, shoulder-width apart, back foot toed outward.

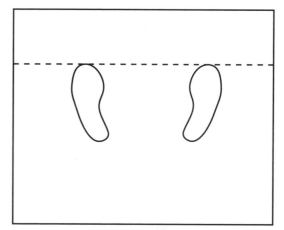

Figure 1.3 The parallel stance (top view). Toe-to-toe relationship, shoulder-width apart.

(see figure 1.2). This position should be used when a player needs to be able to move in any direction.

The parallel stance shown in figure 1.3 is best used for side-to-side movement, as well as for catching the ball and stopping, stopping after dribbling, and responding when a defender moves laterally. In time, players will use both stances interchangeably.

Weight Distribution

Body weight should be evenly distributed from side to side, from front to back, and between feet. Heels should be down, with most of the weight on the balls of the feet, although pressure should be felt on the toes and heels.

Players may incorrectly place all of their weight on the balls of the feet with the heels off the floor, but this position is slower—it requires that the heel be brought down before any forceful movement can take place. A good way to teach the feeling of proper position is to ask players to take an "eagle claw" position, with heels down and toes curled.

When players are on defense, they should add one more thing to their basic position—footfire. This means keeping the feet active and in constant motion without leaving the floor surface, a technique that helps keep leg muscles ready for action. Have players imagine that they are standing on a bed of hot coals, but don't let their feet leave the floor.

Head and Trunk Position

The head is a key to balance because of its relative size and location at the top of the body. Have players keep the head centered over the support base—the head should be the apex of a triangle, with the legs as two equal sides and a line between the feet as the base when seen from the front (figure 1.4). The head is also to be centered from front to back. Players should be taught an erect trunk position with shoulders back and trunk slightly forward of vertical. Keep the head behind the knees.

Critical Cue

Quick stance weight distribution—eagle claw stance, weight on whole foot.

Critical Cue

Defensive quick stance—footfire.

a   b

Figure 1.4a–b (*a*) Head, the key to balance, carried up and alert–the apex of the triangle (front view). (*b*) Side view.

Arms and Legs

Teach players to keep their joints (ankles, knees, hips, shoulders, elbows, and wrists) bent and ready. See figure 1.4b. The hands and arms should be bent and kept close to the body for balance and quickness. Remember, the whole foot bottom should be touching the floor. Remind the players to "stay low"— the angle at the knee joint in back of the legs should be 90° to 120° to maintain a low center of gravity.

Quick stance is used on offense where it often is called a triple-threat position (TT) because the ball is placed on the dominant side of the body near the armpit (pit and protect the ball) where the player can quickly shoot, pass, or dribble. Defensive players also use quick stance by keeping the feet active and arms ready with elbows bent.

Coaching Points for Quick Stance

- Be ready for action; feet ready, hands ready.
- Play and stay low; keep knees bent and head up.
- Get and stay in a quick stance.
- Keep weight on the whole foot with the heels down; eagle claw.

QUICK STARTS, STEPS, TURNS, AND STOPS

Starting, stepping, turning or pivoting, and stopping are the fundamental motions used to move effectively and efficiently in and out of quick stance. These are called offensive and defensive "moves." Remember the coaching rule: teach players to first do it right (execute the skill correctly), then do it quickly, and finally, do it at the right time, every time. Go slow and get a feel for executing the skill properly. Then progressively speed up until a mistake is made. This is called developing game-speed execution.

A player's overall speed is important, but not as critical as quickness (hand-foot speed). As a coach, you need to strive to improve the quickness of each player. Thinking quick and being quick should be your player's constant focus.

Critical Cue

First, do it right, then do it quickly.

Quick Starts

Starting is the first skill your players must learn that uses quick stance. To start quickly, players should shift their weight in the desired direction of movement. For example, to move to the left, body weight is shifted over the left foot by leaning to the left. Remind players that because the head is the key to balance it always leads the weight shift (figure 1.5).

In order to be quick at the right time, players must remember that all motion change begins on the floor. This means taking short, choppy steps whenever a change of motion or quick start is needed. Teach players to keep their feet in contact with the floor as much as possible; teach them that they can use the floor to their advantage by staying close to it, i.e., the floor is a friend—be close to it.

Critical Cue

Think quick and be quick.

Front or Lead Foot First. From basic position, players should shift weight in the direction of movement and start by taking the first step with the nearest foot. For example, to move to the right, the first step is taken with the right foot; to move forward, the first step is with the front foot.

Figure 1.5 Moving laterally left: weight to the desired direction of movement (over left foot).

Critical Cue

Quick steps—play and stay low to the floor (the floor is a friend).

Push Step. On defense, players should use a sliding motion. Have them keep feet at shoulder width and use very short, quick shuffle steps. This technique is called push step. The lead foot points in the direction of desired movement as a short, quick slide step (lead foot first) is taken (figure 1.6). The force for the point and slide step comes from a push from the trail foot, which moves the body and transfers the weight to the lead foot. This is quickly followed by a pulling slide step taken with the trail foot to regain basic position, but do not bring the feet together. Keep feet wide at all times.

Players should learn to execute defensive starts and slides in side-to-side, forward, backward, and diagonal directions (figure 1.7), all done with the head level. Watch for head bouncing; this shows that a player is bouncing along instead of sliding and is not staying in a stance. Such bouncing, known as the "bunny hop," means losing the floor as a friend, and it is a waste of time and space.

Emphasize to players that the head must be kept level. Imagine a "steel plate" above the head—keep head level.

Figure 1.6   Point and push–push step.

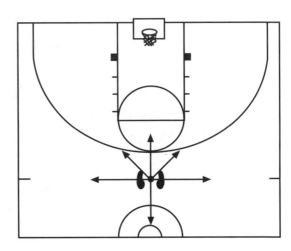

Figure 1.7   Defensive starts and steps directions.

Coaching Points for Quick Starts

- Be ready to start by getting in and maintaining a quick stance.
- Learn that using the floor works to your advantage; keep feet on the floor when starting.
- Shift your weight in the desired direction of movement and lead with the head moving first in that direction.
- Stay down and pump arms when starting.
- Use the principle of front or lead foot first.
- For defensive slides, use the push step technique. Slide, not hop, and keep feet wide.
- Move and start in straight lines.

Quick Steps

Quick steps are the basic motion changes that allow players to use their speed and quickness to complete plays and execute offensive and defensive strategies. They consist of changes of speed or pace and changes of direction (90° and 180°). Quick steps are usually made as "slow to quick" moves.

Change of Pace and Change of Direction.   Change-of-pace steps are important tools of body control designed to apply the concept of "being quick at the right time." These include running/sliding at different speeds, usually a slow-quick pattern called change-of-pace. For example, an offensive player may be running or dribbling at a moderate speed and use a burst of speed to get past the defender. Likewise, a defender could be sliding along and then accelerate quickly to get a legal position in the path of an offensive player to disrupt movement or "take the charge."

Change-of-direction steps are body movements also designed to apply the "being quick at the right time" principle. When running down the floor on offense and needing to change to defense, a player would run, use a stride stop, change direction 180°, and sprint quickly back in the opposite direction. V-cuts are change-of-direction steps at sharp 90° angle moves used on offense or defense. These steps are 90° cuts made by going into the cut slowly, making a sharp-angled change-of-direction move, and accelerating out of the cut quickly. They are sometimes called L cuts and 7 cuts.

Critical Cue

Change-of-pace steps require changes of speed, especially slow-quick moves.

Quick Turns and Pivots

Turning, or pivoting, is motion that rotates the body in a circular fashion around the ball of one foot while the player maintains basic position (figure 1.8). Sixty percent of the weight should be on the pivot foot.

As the basic skill for beginning all motion changes, the pivot or turn is one of the most important player tools for quickness and balance. It is also one of the least used and poorly learned skills in basketball.

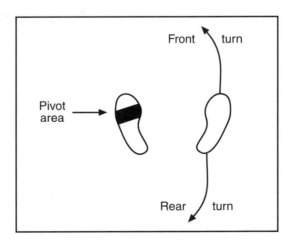

Figure 1.8   Pivoting: a rotation of the body where the ball of the nonpivoting foot remains stationary.

Pivoting can be done on either foot as the stationary center of rotation. When body rotation is toward the front—a pivoting motion that moves the trunk forward around the pivot—the pivot is called a front turn (see figure 1.9). Likewise, a rear turn is used to pivot a player's backside to the rear (figure 1.10). Take your front to the front on a front turn and your rear to the rear on a rear turn.

Players must learn to make pivots with and without the ball on offense. When a player with the ball is closely guarded and wants to face the basket, a rear turn on the nondominant foot as the permanent pivot foot is usually used. On defense, the pivot is the first move that players use when changing from one position to another and when rebounding, as illustrated in figure 1.11. This is sometimes called a swing step.

a   b

Figure 1.9a–b   Right-foot pivot–front turn. *(a)* Starting position and *(b)* ending position.

a   b

Figure 1.10a–b   Left-foot pivot–rear turn. *(a)* Starting position and *(b)* ending position.

Figure 1.11 a–b Defensive rebounding. *(a)* Front turn and *(b)* rear turn, a one-count stop.

Coaching Points for Quick Turns

- Stay down in basic stance and keep the head level.
- Keep feet shoulder-width apart.
- Maintain balance and keep head up.
- Pivot quickly but properly in a quick turn.
- Use the pivot to turn up to a half turn (180°); repeat pivots if more turning is necessary.
- Use a rear turn to face the basket when closely guarded.

Quick Stops

Being quick with balance and control means that players must be able to use quick stance, start properly, move quickly (by running or sliding), and finally stop quickly in a balanced position.

The two recommended basic basketball stops are the one-count "quick stop" and the two-count "stride stop."

Quick Stop. The preferred stop for most situations is the quick stop. Sometimes called the jump stop, the quick stop is executed at the end of a running or sliding motion. When running, a player does a quick stop by jumping slightly from one foot, skimming the floor surface, and landing in a parallel or slightly staggered stance (basic position; see figure 1.12). Both feet hit the floor at the same time in one count.

a   b

Figure 1.12a–b *(a)* Hop from one foot and *(b)* landing in a quick stop (side view).

Critical Cue

Quick stop—hop from one foot, stay close to floor, and land in a quick stance.

The quick stop, a one-count stop, is almost always the preferred stop because it conserves time and space—it takes only one count and occurs quickly, it can be used on defense or offense (with or without the ball), and it is a complement to the quick turn, one of the primary tools of body control and movement. Basketball rules allow players with the ball to use either foot for pivoting after a quick stop. This gives them a wide variety of motion possibilities with control and balance. The quick stop is important for getting into a quick stance for shooting, passing, or dribbling (the triple threat) and can be used very effectively after dribbling or receiving a pass.

The term quick stop is preferred to the jump stop to more properly describe the skill (not jumping into the air and slowly getting into a quick stance).

Stride Stop. The stride stop is a two-count stop executed by landing on the rear foot (first count) with the front foot hitting immediately afterward (second count). Its primary use for all players is to reverse direction when running forward and is best used in other situations for advanced players. For all other motion situations, players should use the quick stop. Keep weight back and sit on the rear foot with the stride stop (figure 1.13).

Coaching Points for Quick Stops and Stride Stops

- Use the quick stop unless changing direction (180°) when running; then use the stride stop.
- When using the quick stop, hop from one foot and land in quick stance on two feet at once. Stay close to the floor.
- Stay low and sit on the back foot when making the stride stop.

Figure 1.13 Stride stop.

Critical Cue

Stride stop—sit on back foot.

QUICK JUMPS

Jumping is an especially important skill in a sport with an elevated goal. Coaches often consider jumping a natural ability that players either have or do not have and a skill that cannot be taught. Nothing could be further from the truth.

There are basic principles for improving jumping skill. First, players need to be taught to be in quick stance ready to jump. When players learn to be ready to jump, then it is possible for them to jump quickly in any situation.

Second, your players will be able to jump higher if they increase the muscle strength in their legs. Coaches should help players improve their leg strength with resistance training as well as working on their jumping skill.

Third, it should be pointed out to players that how they land after a jump will determine how quickly and how high their next immediate jump will be. The best landing position is in a quick stance with balance and a wide base. A player is then ready to jump again. Body position and control are best taught when players have learned first to jump using both feet and both arms.

The sections that follow explain how to execute two-foot jumps, quick jumps, and one-foot jumps, and when to use each one in game situations.

Two-Foot Power Jumps

A two-foot takeoff for jumping is slower but more stable than jumping from one foot on the move. It is best used when players are in high-traffic situations (such as battling a crowd of players for a rebound) or on power lay-ups with close defenders. It is a slower but very strong move from a balanced position.

Critical Cue

Power Jump—two hands, two feet.

The takeoff should be planted firmly before the jump is made (players should visualize themselves stamping their feet through the floor) to provide maximum leg-muscle contraction, i.e., quick stop and jump.

Teach players to use momentum transfer whenever possible, by using the forward momentum of a running jump with forceful contact on the takeoff, and swinging the arms forcefully to add to the body's momentum when time and space permit.

Quick Jumps

Quick jumps are the best compromise between conserving time and space and maintaining body position and control. A quick jump should be used wherever there is congestion, contact, or a contested jump around the basketball. The hands are held head high with the upper arms near horizontal and forearm vertical before a quick jump is made. These are two-foot jumps using two-hands without momentum that start from a quick stance (figure 1.14, figure 1.15).

a   b

Figure 1.14a–b Quick jumps: *(a)* feet ready and *(b)* hands ready.

One-Foot Jumps

Jumping from one foot is beneficial when movement and maximum height are required. Players should know how to do one-foot takeoffs so they can attack the basket on lay-ups and jump high toward the basket or backboard (high jump, not long jump).

a front turn & plant   b   c

Figure 1.15a–c (a) Ready position, (b) quick jump, and (c) return to quick stance.

Coaching Points for Jumps

- Be ready to jump—get in quick stance, jump, and land in quick stance.
- Jump from two feet with two hands most of the time (especially when rebounding) for power jumps and quick jumps.
- Use quick jumps for repeated jumping efforts whenever possible.
- Use a two-foot takeoff for power and control and a one-foot takeoff for speed and height.
- Use momentum transfer from running forward and from the arms swinging upward whenever there is time.
- Use quick stops and quick jumps when shooting a jump shot.

BASIC BODY CONTROL DRILLS

These drills can be used to develop and maintain the basic athletic stance for basketball–quick stance. They also can be used to teach players to move quickly and stop quickly during basketball play. Remember, move with balance and quickness while maintaining control.

Quick Stance Check

PURPOSE

To develop the skill of recognizing various basic stances, getting in a basic stance, and maintaining that stance.

EQUIPMENT

Half-court floor space (minimum).

PROCEDURE

Players spread out on the basketball court facing the coach, assume a basic stance variation as directed, and maintain the stance while it is checked by a coach (or partner). Know the "look" of a quick stance—get in it and stay in it.

Quick Stance Mirror

PURPOSE

To self-evaluate stance variations by recognizing the "look" of a good stance.

EQUIPMENT

Player and full-length mirror.

PROCEDURE

Each player checks all stance variations in front of a mirror, holding each basic stance at least five seconds (front and side view). A partner system also may be used if a mirror is not available.

Line Drill: Quick Starts, Steps, Turns, and Stops

PURPOSE

To develop skill in starting, turning, and stopping.

EQUIPMENT

Full court.

PROCEDURE

All players are divided into four groups behind the baseline at one end of the court with the coach in the middle (figure 1.16). The coach calls out the option players are to perform.

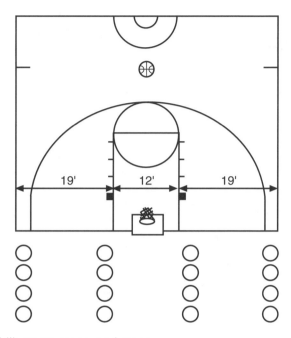

Figure 1.16 Line drill: starts, steps, and stops.

OPTIONS

- All players use a quick start technique from a quick stance.
- Stutter-steps—Start from baseline and go to the opposite end line, keeping the hands up, and making the shoes squeak. Remember to use the floor to your advantage; short, choppy steps.
- Change-of-pace moves—Alternate two or three slow and fast moves after a quick start. Be quick and use a varied number of steps (avoid the same patterns).
- Quick stops—At free-throw line, half-court line, and opposite free-throw line.
- Quick turns—Full front and rear turns (two half turns) after quick stops.
- Split-vision jog—Four players start simultaneously and jog at half speed, focusing on the far basket while using their peripheral vision to stay in a straight line from side to side.
- Stride stops and 180° change of direction.
- Progressive stride stops—Progressive forward and backward moves are made from the baseline to the free-throw line (stride stop, reverse), back to the baseline (reverse), from the baseline to the half-court line (reverse), back to the free-throw line, and then to the opposite free-throw

line, back to the half-court line, and then to the opposite baseline, and so on (figure 1.17).

- Spacing jog (a more advanced skill that also can be used with change-of-pace moves)—The first four players start on command and move at their own paces. The next person in line starts when the player ahead is 15 to 18 feet away (proper spacing between offensive players) and maintains that distance. This is especially challenging in combination with change-of-pace moves.

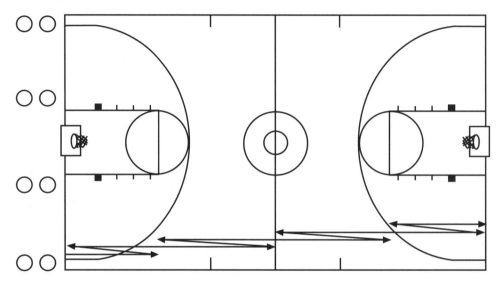

Figure 1.17 Progressive stride stops option.

Coaches may hold players in any quick stop position to check their position and correct mistakes. Players may simulate dribbling a ball or sprinting without the ball (on offense). If defensive quick stops are used, the feet should be active at all times.

The coach can advance to a "whistle stop" drill; four players start and on each short whistle they stride stop (or quick stop), then reverse and sprint until the next whistle. The next group of four players always starts on the second whistle after the previous group. The drill continues until a player reaches the opposite baseline and all players have run the floor. This is an excellent conditioning drill.

DRILL REMINDERS

- Each variation is done in one circuit (down and back).
- The first player in each line should always come to a quick stance position on the baseline and be ready before being required to move. Players should listen for the direction and command "go" from the coach.
- Equal side-to-side floor spacing should be kept when initiating movement.

- Unless directed otherwise, subsequent groups of four begin moving when the previous group reaches the near free throw line (about 15 to 18 feet apart).
- All groups move to the opposite baseline and re-form with the first group of four in quick stance ready to come back in the opposite direction.

Line Drill: Quick Jumps

PURPOSE

To develop basic jumping skills for rebounding and shooting.

EQUIPMENT

Half-court floor space (minimum).

PROCEDURE

Players are in four lines on the baseline with the coach near the half-court line. One "down and back" circuit of quick jumps can be added. The first wave of players sprints forward from basic position on the command "go." Every time a "thumbs-up" signal is given, players execute a quick stop into a quick jump. They continue to repeat quick jumps in place until the coach signals them to run forward again with a "hitchhiking" sign. The first group sprints again as the next group starts from basic position on the end line. This is repeated until all groups reach the opposite end line. The coach must be in front of and visible to all groups so the players can see his or her signals. An alternate is to require three quick jumps at the free throw line, half-court line, and opposite free throw line. A regular power rebound jump and chinning the ball with both hands under the chin can also be done.

Critical Cue

Arms up, hands above the waist.

Line Drill: Rebound Jumping

PURPOSE

To develop jumping skills for rebounding situations.

EQUIPMENT

A ball for each line.

PROCEDURE

Using basic jumping techniques, have a player or coach toss the ball in the air in front of the first player, who jumps and grabs the ball with both hands, puts the ball under the chin (chinit) with elbows out to protect the ball while landing in a quick stance.

Line Drill: Quick Stance/Starts/Steps/Jumps/Turns/Stops

PURPOSE

To develop body control movements by executing all skills properly, quickly, and at the right time. This is an ideal practice warm-up drill.

EQUIPMENT

Full-court floor space.

PROCEDURE

Players in three or four lines on the baseline. Coach is positioned in midcourt area and commands a half or full circuit of body control moves. Players get in and stay in a quick stance, play, and stay low as they execute a variety of combinations as directed by the coach.

2

Advanced Body Control

"Basic basketball (the fundamental skills) is critical to success—this includes learning to *move without the ball*."

—Fred "Tex" Winter, longtime assistant coach, Chicago Bulls

O ne of the most difficult coaching tasks is to teach your players to carry out actions that don't involve the basketball—the magnet of our game. An individual player will be playing without the basketball over 80 percent of the time while on offense (figure 2.1).

This chapter illustrates the considerable importance of developing individual skills that do not involve possession of the basketball. Many coaches believe that this is a problem area with most young players. These players often are "magnetized" by the ball and seem to be almost obsessively attracted to the ball on offense. Considerable time must be spent teaching them that movement without the ball and proper offensive spacing can be just as important in setting up scoring opportunities as moves made with the ball. Helping players understand this is the key to motivating them to carry out purposeful movement when they do not have the ball.

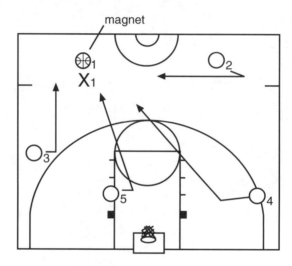

Figure 2.1 Ball magnet and team spacing.

CONCEPTS OF MOVING WITHOUT THE BALL

In order for players to move effectively without the ball, there are certain fundamentals they must master and remember on the court.

- Be alert and remember that all moves begin *on the floor*. The floor is a friend.
- Move with authority, balance, and quickness.
- Move with a purpose. Players must be aware of teammates' movements and maintain their focus on the offensive strategies of the whole team.
- Read the defense and the ball. All individual movement is dictated by the team play situation, but it must be carried out in relation to the position and movement of the ball as well as the opponents' defense. Players must be taught to get open by moving to clear areas on the court where they can receive passes.

- Get open or get out. The primary purpose of movement without the ball is to get open to receive a pass from the ballhandler. Players should learn to first try to get open and then, if this is not possible, to get out of the way. Keep proper spacing of 15 to 18 feet apart.

- Get in the perfect catching position. This is a position 15 to 18 feet from the ballhandler where players are open to receive the ball. Ideally, this also will be in a floor position affording a player the option to pass, shoot, or dribble.

- Be an actor. Movement without the ball is a continuous competition between the offensive and defensive players. Keeping opponents guessing requires using believable fakes to bait the defenders and playing the role of decoy.

- Lose the defender. Move out of the defenders' fields of vision and force them to turn their heads. Since most defenders have their backs to the basket and their eyes on the ball, offensive players should move behind them to the baseline and away from the ball (see figure 2.2). Cuts can best be made from this position because it is difficult for defenders to anticipate moves.

- Run through leather. When moving to catch a pass it is important for players to maintain the "open position" by moving toward and meeting the pass, unless they are making a breakaway move to the basket ahead of the defender or a backcut behind a defender (figure 2.3).

- Get close to get open. Because this rule goes against common sense, many players make the mistake of trying to free themselves by staying away from a defender. It is actually more effective to stay close to the defender and then break away quickly to get open, as seen by O_2 and O_3 in figure 2.4. This move is almost always effective because it allows the offensive player to execute an action move that is made before and is quicker than the defender's reaction move. Action is quicker than reaction. An effective V-cut or L-cut to get open is often a short, quick move.

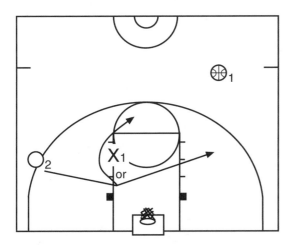

Figure 2.2 Lose the defender (move out of defenders' fields of vision).

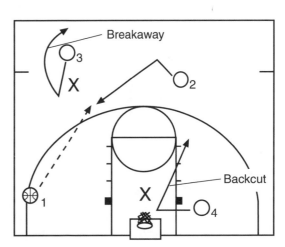

Figure 2.3 Run through leather (meet the pass—O_2).

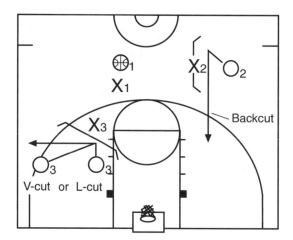

Figure 2.4 Get close to get open. O_3 moves close to X_3, then makes a quick V-cut or L-cut move to get open to receive a pass. O_2 moves toward X_2 who is overplaying the pass from O_1 and O_2 then backcuts to the basket.

BASIC MOVES OR STEPS WITHOUT THE BALL

Basic moves without the ball should be taught to every player. Most of these moves require that the player be deceptive in order to fool the defense. Remember, go slow first and be correct, then be progressively quicker.

V-Cuts

Critical Cue

Use V-cuts (fake and break) to get open.

Special-purpose cuts or moves (quick steps) will also include "fake-and-break," or V-cuts (basic zigzag or change-of-direction cuts that form the shape of a V). To execute a V-cut, place weight on the foot opposite the desired direction (sink the hips into the cut), point the lead foot, and step with this opposite foot. For example, plant and push from the right foot and step to the left with the left foot. One side of the V is usually the move to the basket, away from the basket, or to the defender. The other side of the V is the quick change-of-direction cut to get open. Young players can be taught this best by using the term fake-and-break for the V-cut to get open. The first part of the V-move to the basket or the defender (the fake) is done slowly and is quickly followed by the last part of the V (the break) to get open. On the break, both hands are thrown up and in the direction of movement. The break move is usually toward the ball but can be toward the basket as in O_2's backcut move on X_2's overplay (figure 2.4).

Front and Rear Cuts

These are moves made after a player has passed the ball to a teammate and wants to challenge the defense by cutting to the basket for a possible return pass. The pass-and-cut move—sometimes called "give-and-go" basketball—is one of the most valuable offensive moves in the game.

The give-and-go takes two forms: the preferred front cut, which allows the offensive player to receive the ball in front of the defender (an excellent

scoring position), and the rear cut, which lets the offensive player cut behind the defender to gain an advantage going to the basket (figure 2.5).
Note that a front cut uses a V-cut to set up the defense whereas the rear cut
is a direct, straight-line cut, as a change-of-pace or slow-quick move. Both
front and rear cuts are cuts "to the rim" that end exactly in front of the
basket.

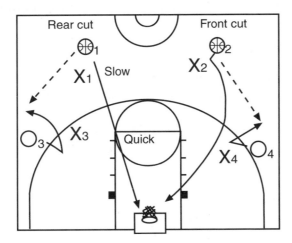

Figure 2.5 Front and rear cuts—give-and-go basketball.

Decoy Moves

Decoy moves are any of the basic moves used to keep defenders busy, such as
distracting defensive players from helping to defend against a ballhandler or
to trap the ball. Teach players to be actors and distracters, misleading defenders with deceptive eye movements, physical bluffs, and other visual or audi-
tory distractions.

Shot Moves

When the ball is in the air on a shot attempt by the offensive team, each offensive player should either move to a rebounding position or go to a defensive
assignment, depending upon their position. Players should be taught to make
decisive moves when a shot is taken. Do not stand and watch the ball. Spectators are ball watchers, players are movers. Always assume the shot will be
missed and either rebound or get back on defense.

Assigned Moves

Assigned moves are individually assigned cuts in a system of play for special
situations. Coaches make these specific assignments for jump balls, out-of-
bounds plays, free throws, and set patterns. All players must carry out individual assignments properly and quickly. How well this is done is just as important as what is being done. All cuts need to be done quickly and at the right
time. Execution is more important than what move is done.

SCREEN MOVES

Setting and using screens to get a teammate open for a pass or a drive is one of the most unselfish team moves that players can learn. This also includes being able to use screens as an essential skill of individual offense. Instruction in setting and using screens should begin at the secondary level—elementary school players should concentrate on learning other moves without the ball.

Types of Screens

Screens can be classified according to location (on the ball or away from the ball), how they are used (back [back to the basket] screens that are set behind or on the blind side of a defender and down screens [back to the ball] that are set in front of or to the side of a defender), and by the kind of body contact used to screen (front or rear of body). See figure 2.6.

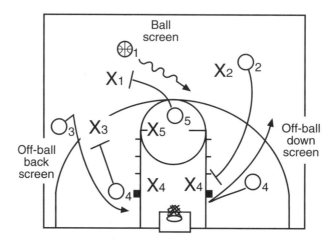

Figure 2.6 Types of screens.

Coaches should develop their own theories of how screens should work. Some coaches advocate screening a certain spot or area on the floor (position screen), whereas others believe in screening the defender (player screen). A player screen is usually more effective in freeing the offensive player but may result in more fouls being charged for illegal screens, or *blocks*. The authors prefer player screens; screen an opponent, not a spot or a teammate.

Setting Screens

Setting a screen is a basic move that should be taught as follows. Players should use a noisy, quick stop with the feet shoulder-width apart and the hands out of the screen (figure 2.7). The screen should be set perpendicular to the expected path of the defender and should be forceful enough for the defender to see and hear it. Screening players should be loud, low, and legal. A loud, low screen is one set with a good quick stance after a quick stop. You can hear it being set and when the defender makes contact with it. Play and stay low—be ready for contact. Finally, the screen should be legal—correct position and legal use of hands. A down screen can be set skin-to-skin, but a back screen must allow at least one step for the defender to change direction. To avoid illegal hand contact, one hand should grasp the other wrist and the hands are placed in front of the body over vital parts. Against good defensive teams the cutter will usually be covered, but the screener will often be open when a defensive switch or help is made.

a   b

Figure 2.7a–b Front screen: noisy quick stop with wide base, keeping arms out of screen. *(a)* Men, *(b)* women.

Other tips on screening include using down screens (toward the basket) against "sagging" defenders and back screens (away from the basket) against pressure or "over-playing" defenders.

Be ready for contact and screen the defender.

Using Screens

The most difficult screening skill is to prepare the defender to run into the screen (players should use a teammate as a screen or obstacle) with a V-cut, usually started toward the basket as shown in figure 2.8. An important cue is to wait-wait-wait for the screen.

Players should cut "razor close" to the screener, so that they brush shoulder to shoulder with the screener. On screens away from the ball, players using a screen should be in quick stance as they pass the screen with hands up, ready to receive a pass. Throw your hands up as you move past the screener on the "break." Timing is a crucial factor in effective screen plays; players must wait for the screen to be set before making their moves.

Critical Cue

Set loud, low, and legal screens.

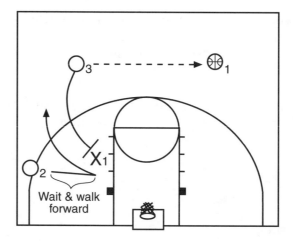

Figure 2.8 Using the screen. Wait-wait-wait (O_2) as the V-cut is made.

On-the-Ball Screens

The "pick-and-roll" is a basic two-person play used at all levels of basketball. This play is a staple for one of the best inside-outside combinations in basketball history–Karl Malone and John Stockton of the Utah Jazz. This play occurs when a screen is set on the ballhandler. When an effective screen is used and defenders do not switch, the dribbler will be open for a shot (dribble drive lay-up or set/jump shot) as seen in figure 2.9. The sequence occurs as O_1 V-cuts to get open as O_2 passes and sets the ball screen on defender X_1. In this option, X_1 tries to fight through the screen (defenders do not switch assignments), is impeded, and O_1 is free for the shot (lay-up or set/jump).

When a screen (pick) is made on the ballhandler and the defenders switch assignments, the screener will be open on a "roll" move to the basket. The "pick-and-roll" move for the screener is shown in figure 2.10. The screen is set

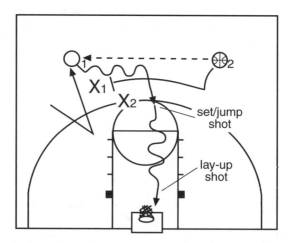

Figure 2.9 Pick-and-roll–defenders stay (no switched assignments).

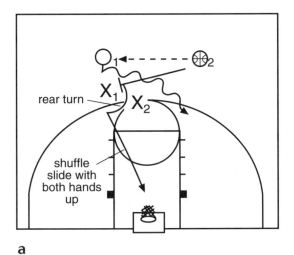

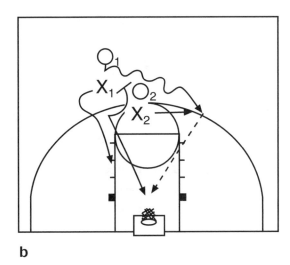

a

b

Figure 2.10a–b Pick-and-roll–defenders switch. *(a)* Screen (pick) set and rear turn on left foot as dribbler clears screen, *(b)* roll-pass to screener rolling to the basket.

and used. When the ballhandler uses the screen, the screener makes a *half* rear turn and shuffle slides to the basket, keeping between the ballhandler and the original defender X_1. The ballhandler must make at least two dribbles past the screen to "draw" the switching defender X_2 and then a pass (usually a bounce) is made to the screener on the roll move to the basket.

On all screen plays, there are always two possible scoring options when an effective screen is made: the nonscreener is open if defenders don't switch, and the screener is open if the defenders switch. Advanced players should be taught to look for both scoring options.

Another advanced option on all two-person screen plays is for the screener to "slip the screen" or fake the screen and cut to the basket as the defenders choose to switch defensive assignments in early anticipation of the screen. This option for on-the-ball screens is shown in figure 2.11.

Critical Cue

Always look for two scoring options on all screen plays—cutter first and screener second.

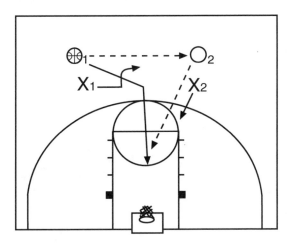

Figure 2.11 Slip the screen.

Off-the-Ball Screens

This type of screen is set *away from* the ball and occurs as a basic two-player pattern plus the passer. Off-the-ball screens are classified by the cutter's reaction to the defender's choice of combatting the screen:

• A pop cut is used when the defender attempts to fight through the screen (figure 2.12). O_1 passes to O_2 and screens away from the ball *on the defender* of O_3, X_3. O_3 will get an open shot outside if no defensive switch is made (option a). If X_1 switches defensive assignments, the screener O_1 will get the open shot inside by cutting to the ball as the switch is made (option b).

• A curl cut is used when the defender trails the cutter around the screen (figure 2.13). In the first option, defense stays, and the cutter gets the open shot inside (curling to the basket). When the defenders switch, the screener O_1 will get the outside shot cutting to the ball (option b). Larry Bird, former Boston Celtic and Hall of Fame player, executed this screen cut to perfection.

• A flare cut is used when the defender anticipates the pop cut (figure 2.14). When the defenders stay (no switch), the cutter will be open by flaring away from the ball and outside (option a). When the defenders switch, the screener will be open (option b) on the inside flash cut to the ball.

• A back cut is used when the cutter makes a pop cut, and the defender fights through the screen (figure 2.15). In option a (no-switch defense), the cutter makes the pop cut, is overplayed, and reacts by making a cut to the basket using the backscreen of O_1. The movement sequence for the cutter is to the basket (in), pop cut (out), and back cut (in) to the basket. When no switch is made, the cutter gets the shot inside going to the basket. In option b (switching defense), the screener O_1 will get the shot flashing to the ball outside as the switch is made.

Movement Mistakes. Movement mistakes occur when a player without the ball commits an error. Teach players to focus their attention on recovery, call out for help from teammates when needed, and get in position for the next play immediately. This is especially important when an offensive error results in a steal. Avoid making two mistakes in a row. Learn to play through mistakes.

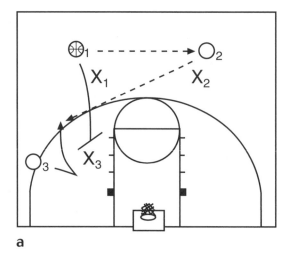

a

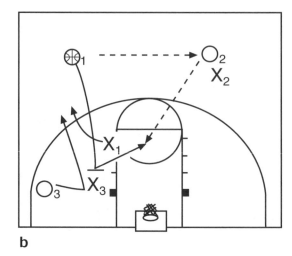

b

Figure 2.12a–b Pop cut. *(a)* No-switch defense, *(b)* switching defense.

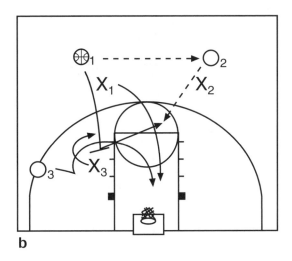

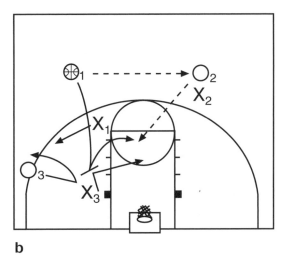

Figure 2.13a–b Curl cut. *(a)* No-switch defense, *(b)* switching defense.

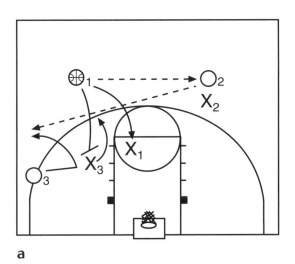

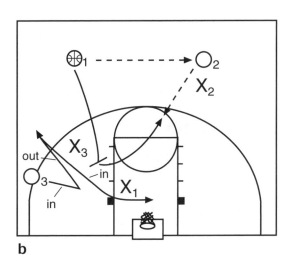

Figure 2.14a–b Flare cut. *(a)* No-switch defense, *(b)* switching defense.

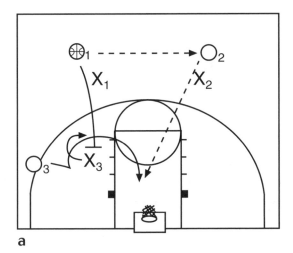

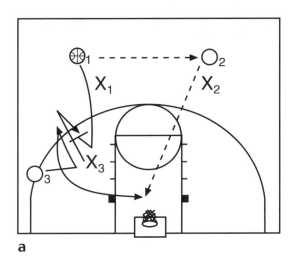

Figure 2.15a–b Back cut. *(a)* No-switch defense, *(b)* switching defense.

Coaching Points for Moving Without the Ball

- Use the floor when beginning a move.
- Move with authority.
- Move with a purpose.
- Read the defense and the ball and react.
- Get open or get out of the way; don't stand still.
- Know and use the perfect catching position (15–18 feet from the ball).
- Be an actor: take the initiative, use believable fakes.
- Lose the defender.
- Run through leather (meet the pass).
- Get close to get open.
- Set loud, low, and legal screens.
- Set picks or screens at right angles to expected path of defender.
- When using screens, wait-wait-wait, use V-cuts, brush past screen.
- Pick and roll: the two scoring options for on-the-ball screens.
- Off-the-ball screen cuts: pop, curl, flare, and back.
- Two scoring options on every screen—cutter and screener.

BASIC DRILLS FOR MOVING WITHOUT THE BALL

These drills are designed to teach players the most challenging moves, those without the ball. Players tend to be eager to develop "ball" skills and more reluctant to drill on moves without the ball.

Line Drill: Moves Without the Ball

PURPOSE

To teach basic moves without the ball by simulation.

EQUIPMENT

Half court (minimum).

PROCEDURE

The players should assume a basic four-line drill position on the baseline. The first player in each line moves down the court without the ball, imagining the ball to be in the center of the court (figure 2.16).

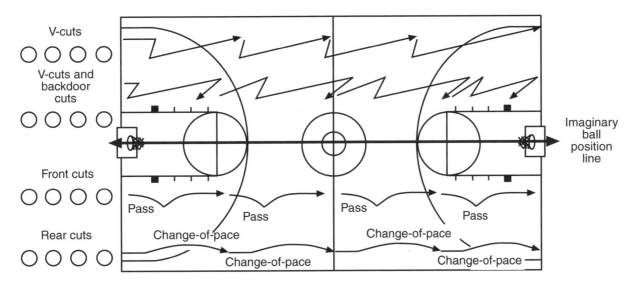

Figure 2.16 Line drill: V-cuts, backdoor cuts, front cuts, and rear cuts without the ball.

OPTIONS

- V-cuts to get open (designated to the basket and to the ball or to the defender and to the ball)—repeated V-cuts followed by quick stops to simulate catching the ball performed for the length of the court.
- V-cut to get open followed by a backdoor cut. Proper footwork and hand position are emphasized (keep hands up—get open; outside hand down—backdoor).
- Front cuts—a simulated pass to the center of the court is followed by a front cut (V-cut, slow move away, fast cut to the ball) and quick stop at the free throw lines and the half-court line.
- Rear cuts—a simulated pass to the center of the court is followed by a rear cut (change-of-pace; slow to fast) and quick stop at the free throw lines and the half-court line.

Quick stops are used at each free throw line and the half-court line. At the completion of each quick stop, players should challenge the imaginary defense by using a "catch-and-face" move: first quick stop, then pivot and face the basket, seeing the whole court.

V-Cut Drill

PURPOSE

To teach players the basic moves without the ball in a two-on-zero, two-on-two situation.

EQUIPMENT

One ball per basket per group.

PROCEDURE

The basic two-line formation for this drill is one line of guards or point position players out front and a line of forwards or wing position players on the side, i.e., two lines of outside players.

OPTIONS

- Forwards V-cut to get open (fake and break) and after receiving the pass from the guard, catch and face the basket.
- Guard makes front or rear cut to basket (cut to the rim) and goes to the end of the forward V-cut line (give and go) or the forward can make a live ball, dribble drive move to the basket (figure 2.17a).
- Forward then passes to next guard in line and goes to the end of the guard line.
- Figure 2.17b shows a forward "backdoor" move (advanced skill) performed during a guard dribble move. Key—ballhandler dribbling toward overplaying defender keys backdoor cut or receiver with outside hand down keys the cut (figure 2.18).

The forward V-cut may be a fake to the basket and break to get open or to the imaginary defender (L-cut). When acceptable skill levels are reached, add two defenders and execute the drills in a two-on-two situation.

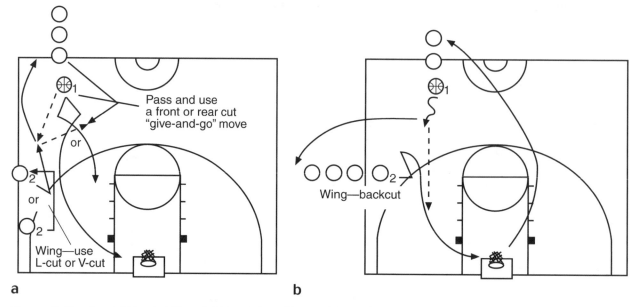

a   b

Figure 2.17a–b   (a) V-cut drill and (b) backdoor. V-cut with outside hand down as key O_2.

Figure 2.18a–b *(a)* Ball "catcher" hand position when open, both hands up, *(b)* straight arm away from defender, with closed fist. When overplayed, outside hand down to key the backdoor cut.

ADVANCED DRILLS FOR MOVING WITHOUT THE BALL

Pick-and-Roll Drill

PURPOSE

To teach players the screening and cutting options for screens on the ball.

EQUIPMENT

One ball per basket per group (four or more).

PROCEDURE

Two lines of outside players 15–18 feet apart using the screening pattern of pass and screen the ballhandler's defender. The progression should be

- Two-on-zero:

    cutter (dribbler) scoring option alternating with the screener scoring option (roll or step outside for shot)

- Two-on-two:

    defense stays (score on the pick) alternating with the defense switches (score on the roll or step outside for shot)

    live offense and defense

    player rotation—offense to defense to the end of the opposite line

• Three-on-three:

live offense and defense

make it, take it (offense keeps the ball when they score; rotate when defense stops the offense)

Three-on-Three Motion Screen Drill

PURPOSE

To teach players the screening and cutting options for screens off the ball.

EQUIPMENT

One ball per basket per group (six or more). You can use two balls to pass on both scoring options.

PROCEDURE

Three lines of outside players 15-18 feet apart using the pass and screen away from the ball options; pop cut, curl cut, flare cut, back cut. The progression should be:

• Three-on-zero:

pop cut (cutter score outside, screener score inside)

curl cut (cutter score inside, screener score outside)

flare cut (cutter score outside, screener score inside)

back cut (cutter score inside, screener score outside)

• Three-on-three:

defense stays (cutter options)

defense switches (screener options)

live offense and defense

make it-take it

3

Ballhandling

> "Passing-catching is an offensive *team* skill, while dribbling is an *individual* offensive skill; therefore the pass should be the primary offensive weapon."
>
> **— Ralph Miller, Hall of Fame coach**

allhandling encompasses all offensive moves with the basketball—passing, catching, dribbling, shooting, individual moves, and rebounding. For our purposes, this chapter's discussion of ballhandling includes only the skills of passing, catching, and dribbling.

The arm mechanics of the ballhandling skills of passing, dribbling, and shooting are almost identical—the arm and hand motion is the same for each skill. Passing and catching are the most important of all the individual offensive fundamentals with the ball, with shooting considered as a pass to the basket. Dribbling is a secondary offensive weapon that never should be misused or overused.

Another ballhandling practice principle must be applied in order to achieve balanced development of dominant and nondominant hand ballhandling skills. Players need to work on their weak hand *twice* as much as on their strong hand.

Getting into triple-threat position (offensive quick stance), where a player with the ball may shoot, pass, or dribble, should become an automatic action (see figure 3.1). Note that in triple-threat (TT) position the player with the ball "pits and protects" the ball (pulls the ball close to the armpit in order to protect it from the defender). The underlying concept is that players, when they become ballhandlers, should first look to pass the ball to a teammate (unless open themselves for a scoring opportunity within range) before choosing to dribble—the final option for moving the ball.

PASSING AND CATCHING

Passing and catching are the most neglected fundamentals in basketball. It is essential that players develop these skills in order to mount a successful team offense. Effective passing and receiving in the form of the scoring assist is a

Critical Cue

Practice nondominant side ballhandling skills (pass, dribble) *twice* as much as dominant side ballhandling skills.

Critical Cue

Get in triple-threat—pit and protect the ball and face your basket using a front or rear turn.

Figure 3.1 Triple-threat position (offense quick stance with the ball).

measure of the degree of offensive teamwork and also can be an important tool for controlling game tempo on offense.

Ensure that players who are good passers and receivers have an excellent chance to be important team members. From a coaching standpoint, good passing tends to take the pressure off a team's defensive play and to break down the opponent's defense. Because passing is the quickest way to move the ball and challenge the defense, it should be the primary weapon of your team's offensive attack.

Earvin "Magic" Johnson led his college and NBA teams to championships by becoming one of the greatest passers in the history of the game.

Develop the notion that passing and catching are the best offensive team plays by explaining that they are the most effective way of achieving the offensive objective—getting the ball to an open player to set up a scoring opportunity.

PASSING PRINCIPLES

Players need to look for the pass *before* dribbling. A player's first instinct when catching the ball is to dribble, and only continual emphasis on the pass will change this. Since dribbling is an individual skill practiced each time a player touches the ball, a natural preference for dribbling tends to develop.

There are a number of other fundamental elements of passing that should be taught. Good passes only can be made when these factors are present:

- Quickness—the ball must be passed quickly (before the defender has time to react). The pass should be snappy and crisp, but not too hard or too easy. A quick step is usually made in the direction of the pass—this provides added force. When a quick pass is thrown, a "ping" sound is heard. When thrown too hard, the pass slaps loudly as it is caught; when thrown too soft, no sound is heard when the pass is caught.

- A target—each pass must be thrown accurately to a specific target (usually away from the defender). A raised hand or shoulder away from the defender is commonly used as the target.

- Timing—the ball must be delivered when the receiver is open and not before or after.

- Trickery—the passer must use deception to confuse the defender, who is reading the passer (especially the eyes) and anticipating the pass.

Passers should visually locate all teammates on the court as well as defenders, concentrating on the potential receiver without staring. This can best be done by surveying the whole floor area with the ball in triple-threat position. When they catch a pass, players should always be prepared to shoot when open and within range; if unable to shoot themselves, they should try to pass to an open teammate before dribbling.

Players must learn to give up the ball unselfishly by passing to an open player. Ballhandlers also can dribble drive and pass (penetrate and pitch)—they can create an opportunity for an assist by making a dribble move that allows them to pass to a open teammate to score. When players are passing, the choice should be to make the easy pass through or by the defender. Teach players not to gamble on passes. They should be clever, not fancy.

Critical Cue

See the whole floor, look to pass first, dribble last.

Critical Cue

Pass with a ping. This concept was made popular by Fred "Tex" Winter, longtime assistant for the Chicago Bulls.

Critical Cue

Make the easy pass.

Critical Cue

Pass with feet on the floor—catch passes with feet in the air.

John Stockton, Gonzaga University and Utah Jazz All-Star player, has become the all-time assist record holder by "making the easy pass."

Finally, passes should be made with both feet on the floor and received with feet in the air. Pass with feet on the floor—catch with feet in the air. This means just barely get the feet off the floor—put a little air under the feet. The receiver then catches the ball with two hands and quickly moves the ball to the TT quick stance position.

Choosing the Correct Pass

The quickest passes are air passes. Simple geometry (the shortest distance between two points is a straight line) proves that the air pass is quicker than either the lob pass or the bounce pass, as shown in figure 3.2. Therefore, the air pass is the primary pass to use. All perimeter passes around the defense should be air passes.

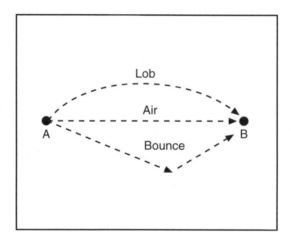

Figure 3.2 Types of passes—their path and distance traveled.

Lob passes are used only when passing to teammates on a breakaway fast break and the lob allows them to run to catch up with the ball, when teammates are being fronted while playing a low post position, or when this is the best way to get the ball past a defender.

Bounce passes are used only when passing to

- players in the post position who are smaller than the defender,
- post players open on the baseline side,
- players making a backdoor cut, or
- players in an emergency.

Special Passing Situations

Other aspects related to passing also must be covered. These include eliminating the pass across under the defensive basket—an interception there usually results in a score by the opponents. Other danger areas for catching the ball are along boundary lines and in court corners as shown (figure 3.3). When a pass comes back out on the perimeter from the baseline, players should

Figure 3.3 Passing danger areas.

reverse the ball quickly to the other side of the court to test the defense and check for the opponents' alertness on the help side of the defense.

TYPES OF PASSES

There are several types of passes used in basketball. The pass used must fit each particular situation.

Chest Pass

The chest pass is the basic air pass for effective, efficient ball movement when an offensive player is loosely guarded. The starting position for the pass is reached by moving the ball from triple-threat position to the center of the chest close to the body in a "thumbs-up" position. To throw the pass, a player then extends the elbows and pronates (rotates outward) the arms to a "thumbs-down" ending position. Remind players to push the thumbs through the ball to produce backspin on the ball. Players should take a step forward to pass when there is time, but passing without stepping is quicker. The target of the pass is the receiver's throat (neck) area when he or she is stationary and toward the receiver's outside hand or shoulder when he or she is near a defender.

Critical Cue

Chest pass—thumbs up to thumbs down.

Bounce Pass

This pass is recommended primarily for backdoor moves and emergencies when the passer must get out of a trap or when the defender is playing in the passing lane. Passing tips include making the pass to a target two-thirds of the way to the receiver and following through to that spot on the floor. The technique used is the same as for a chest pass. The pass should be thrown hard enough that it bounces up to the receiver at hip level. Starting with the ball in a thumbs-up position, passers should push the thumbs through the ball and follow through to a thumbs-down position. The backspin is important in this movement because it increases the angle of rebound on the bounce pass, making it easier to handle (figure 3.4). Players also may step forward with the pass when there is time.

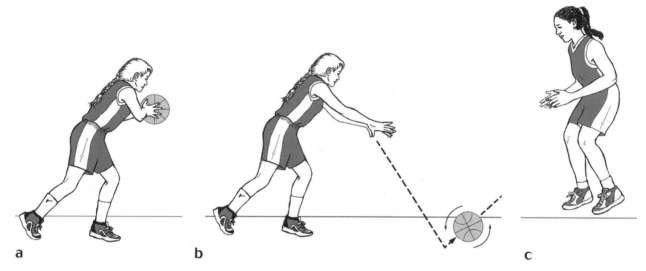

a   b   c

Figure 3.4a–c Bounce pass: *(a)* thumbs-up starting position (target is spot on the floor), *(b)* thumbs-down ending position (follow through to the spot), and *(c)* note catcher with feet in the air.

Overhead Pass

When a player catches the ball it is always moved quickly to TT position. The ball can then be moved quickly overhead to pass over the defense. This is a valuable pass over the defense; it is especially effective against zone defenses. The position of the ball allows the passer to show the ball and use pass fakes. Teach players to keep the ball up—they should start with and keep elbows locked or extended. The pass is thrown with the wrists and fingers—the ball should be overhead with no windup behind the head.

The technique involves starting with thumbs back, then pushing thumbs through the ball, and finishing with thumbs forward (figure 3.5). The overhead pass has a tendency to drop so the ball should be thrown to a high target (usually the receiver's head); the pass is hard to handle when it is dropping. For more power, players should step forward with the pass.

a   b

Figure 3.5a–b Overhead pass: (a) thumbs-back starting position (ball up, elbows locked), and (b) thumbs forward (use wrist and fingers, keep ball up).

Critical Cue

Overhead pass—thumbs back to thumbs forward, ball up, elbows locked.

Baseball Pass

A baseball pass is used to throw a long pass (usually over half-court length). The essential teaching points are as follows: Players should keep two hands on the ball as long as possible. They should use a stance with the body parallel to the sidelines, feet parallel to the baseline, and then plant the back foot, point and step with the front foot, and throw the ball from the ear, similar to a baseball catcher's throw. Proper follow-through includes carrying out a full pronation and extension of the arm ending with the thumb down (figure 3.6). Players should throw this pass only with the dominant arm, using the off hand to catch the fake pass and stabilize the ball.

Critical Cue

Baseball pass—both hands on the ball.

a   b   c

Figure 3.6a–c Baseball pass: (a) starting position—by the ear, both hands on the ball, (b) pull the string—the fake pass can be used from this position, and (c) pronate (thumbs down) on release.

One-Hand Push Pass

Critical Cue

Use push pass when closely guarded.

The one-hand push pass (flip) is the most important offensive pass. It is a quick pass used to pass through or by a closely guarding defender. It may be an air or bounce pass and should be used from the triple-threat position; the key is the bent-elbow starting position. The passer should work one side of the defender's body, especially past the ear, where the biggest gap usually appears. The pass is made above or below the defender's arms after finding an opening through which to pass. Vertical fakes are used as players "read" the defense (figure 3.7). Players should fake low and pass high (air pass) or fake high (maybe a shot fake) and pass low (bounce pass)—read the defender's arm position and make short, quick fakes.

a   b   c

Figure 3.7a–c Push pass: *(a)* triple-threat position, *(b)* work one side of the defender's body, the hole by the ear, and *(c)* use vertical fakes.

CATCHING PRINCIPLES

Catching the basketball requires a player to be ready—potential pass receivers should be in a quick stance position with both hands up. They must be open and give a target at the right time.

"Run through leather" is another receiving rule that means to meet the pass unless the player is cutting to the basket on a backdoor cut or a breakaway situation. When defended, the receiver must move toward the ball until contact is made to ensure possession. Make a cut to finish "running through leather" about 15–18 feet from the ball.

Players should catch the ball with feet slightly in the air whenever possible. The receiver should catch the ball with both feet in the air and come to a quick stop. This ensures body control, ball possession, and a quick return to quick stance where either foot can be used as the pivot foot.

Playing two-handed basketball is a good habit to develop in your players. They should always catch the ball with both hands. There are three methods of catching the ball. The first is with two hands up (thumbs together), used when the pass is near the middle of the body and above the waist (figure 3.8). The second is with two hands down (thumbs apart), used when the pass is near the middle of the body and below the waist (figure 3.9). The third method is the block and tuck, used when the pass is to either side of the body. The ball is blocked with one hand and tucked with the other hand. Both hands should be placed on the ball immediately (figure 3.10).

The receiver should let the wrist and elbows give as the pass is caught. This is sometimes called developing "soft hands." Another tip: The eyes should be focused on the pass until it is in both hands. Tell players to "catch the ball with their eyes" by "looking" the ball into their hands.

Figure 3.8 Two-hands-up catch for passes above waist. Catch the ball with the wrist back, be ready to shoot.

Figure 3.9 Two-hands-down catch for passes near the middle of the body and below the waist.

Coaching Points for Passing and Catching

- Teach triple-threat (TT) position; pit and protect the ball.
- Help passers develop quickness, use of a target, and timing.
- Pass with feet on the floor.
- Teach players to pass and catch with two hands whenever possible.
- Teach players to catch the ball with their feet in the air, watch the ball until it is in their hands, and land with a quick stop.
- Players should learn to catch and immediately scan and see the whole court.
- Train catchers to be ready for bad passes.

a   b

Figure 3.10a–b   (a) Block and (b) tuck for passes to the side.

Pass-Catch Communication

It is the responsibility of both passer and catcher to complete each pass. Strive for perfection and settle for success. Successful passes depend on communication, especially by the catcher. Every potential pass receiver should always be ready to catch a pass (quick stance/hands up) and should call the passer's name to tell them he or she is open. The passer still must decide whether to make the pass.

DRIBBLING

Dribbling is a touch skill, not a sight skill. Players should learn to dribble up the court without watching the ball. This can be accomplished by focusing on the offensive basket while dribbling and looking over the whole court (using peripheral vision). "Seeing the net" will allow the dribbler to see the court and open teammates. The primary objective is to create a move that allows a player to pass to a teammate for a score. Situations for dribbling are the live ball move, a basket penetration move past an opponent using the dribble drive to the basket, and ball movement to get a teammate open. Dribbling is also an acceptable option for advancing the ball up the court when a pass is not available, maneuvering for better position for a pass to a teammate, executing an offensive play or pattern, and getting out of heavy defensive traffic or a defensive trap situation (two defenders on the dribbler).

Dribbling Technique

The dribble is executed by first extending the elbow and flexing the wrist and fingers. Dribble with the wrist, hand, and a little forearm motion. The ball is

Critical Cue

Catchers—get open, be ready, call for the ball, catch ball with feet in air.

Critical Cue

Dribble to make a live ball move, penetrate the defense, get a teammate open, advance the ball, execute a play, or get out of trouble.

controlled by the fingers and pads of the hand (the ball should be kept off the heel of the hand); the fingers are spread comfortably and should be cupped around the ball (figure 3.11). Massage the ball, but dribble it firmly.

Critical Cue

Dribbling is a touch skill; see the net and the whole court.

a   b

Figure 3.11a–b Dribbling: *(a)* use fingers and pads of hands, *(b)* elbow flexion, and wrist-finger to push.

It is important to maintain maximum contact with the ball. The rules of basketball require that the hand stay on top of the ball; the dribble is legal as long as the hand does not leave its vertical position to get under and carry the ball (figure 3.12a). The ball also must leave the dribbler's hand before the pivot foot leaves the floor when starting a legal dribble (figure 3.12b).

Critical Cue

Dribble mostly with the wrist and hand.

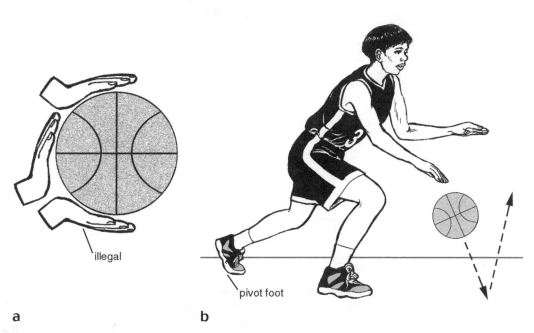

illegal

pivot foot

a   b

Figure 3.12a–b Dribbling rules: *(a)* hand position, *(b)* legal dribble.

Critical Cue

To protect the ball when dribbling in traffic, use a quick stop and *chin the ball* (chin-it).

It is strongly recommended that the quick stop be used to terminate the dribble (figure 3.13). This stop is commonly thought to be the best method of avoiding traveling violations and protecting the ball while conserving critical time and space for passing or shooting. When in traffic, pick up the dribble, use a quick stop, and chin the ball.

When chinning the ball, get in a quick stance with the ball under the chin—fingers up, elbows out (make yourself big).

Players should learn to use either hand to dribble. Help them develop the weak hand but use the preferred hand whenever possible. They always should use the dribbling hand away from the defender when closely guarded. Teach players to protect the ball with the body and the opposite hand (arm bar) when dribbling against a close defender. They should keep the ball low and to the side of the body, and stay in a quick stance (figure 3.14).

Figure 3.13 Terminate the dribble with a quick stop.

Figure 3.14 Closely guarded dribbler: protect the ball with the body and opposite hand, keep tension on legs, and stay in quick stance.

Dribbling Strategies

When the ball is put on the floor the dribbler always should be going somewhere with a purpose. This is a general dribbling rule. On drives to the basket, the dribbler goes past the defender. The objective is to use one dribble to score; bouncing the ball once or dribbling while not changing floor position (called "dropping" the ball) should be discouraged. A dribble penetration (penetrate and pitch) is best accomplished just after receiving a pass; this avoids forcing the dribble into defenders who are prepared for the penetration.

Another key guideline is to stay away from trouble while dribbling. Players should avoid dribbling into traffic (between two defenders) and keep alert for traps by watching for defenders and avoiding the corners of the court when dribbling (figure 3.15).

Players should keep the dribble under control and conclude a dribble with a pass or shot, preferably after a quick stop. A dribbler should use the right move at the right time and see the whole court ahead as well as teammates and defenders.

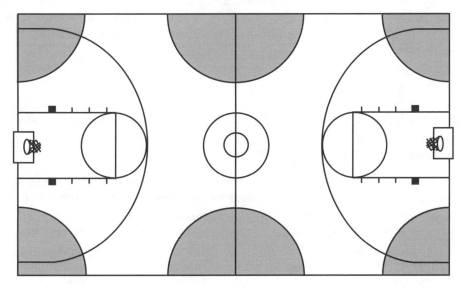

Figure 3.15 Stay out of trouble with the ball—avoid the corners of the basketball court.

Dribble Moves

The right type of dribble should be used at the right time. A low or control dribble should be used around defenders when the dribbler is closely guarded and a high or speed dribble should be used in the open court when advancing the ball. All dribble moves should change directions at sharp angles.

Low Dribble. A control or low dribble is the first and easiest dribble to teach your players. They should use a staggered stance, bent knees with the ball-side foot back. The opposite hand (arm bar) is used for protection from the defender. It cannot be used to push the defender back or hook the defender but only to protect the ball. The basic body motion is a sliding movement similar to defensive slides or a short step running motion.

Players should protect the ball by dribbling on the side of the body away from the defensive player and keeping the ball low.

Critical Cue

Power dribble when using a dribble against extreme defensive pressure.

Power Dribble. An advanced version of the low/control dribble is the power dribble. This is executed by using a sliding foot motion and low dribble so that the ball is protected by the front leg and hip/front arm bar. The ball is dribbled knee high behind the back leg as far away from the defender as possible. The dribbler advances up the court with defensive push step moves. From this position a player can use advanced dribble moves (described later), such as a pull-back crossover, a spin dribble or a fake spin dribble to create space and attack the basket. Vision should be maintained up the floor over the lead shoulder.

Speed Dribble. A speed or high dribble is taught next. Players should push the ball out in front and run after it, keeping it ahead of them. The ball can be dribbled higher—near waist level—to attain more speed. The faster the movement, the farther out in front and the higher the ball should be dribbled.

Change-of-Pace Dribble. A change-of-pace move is accomplished by changing speeds from a low or control dribble in a stop-and-start motion. When slowing or stopping, dribblers should straighten up slightly to relax the defender. This move should be used to move past defenders who take the "slow pace" or "stop" fake. This is another slow-fast move to get dribblers in the clear and keep them open.

On the change-of-pace or hesitation dribble, you can make it look like you are going to shoot or pass as you straighten up or hesitate. If within shooting range, fake pulling up for a jump shot; if out of shooting range, look to the other side of the court as if you are raising up to pass to that side.

Critical Cue

Cross over quick, low, and close to body.

Crossover Dribble. A crossover or switch dribble is a basic move used in the open court when there is sufficient room between the dribbler and defender, and the dribbler has momentum to move by the defender (figure 3.16). Never cross over on a stationary defender. Attack one side of the defender and use the crossover dribble when the defender has stopped your initial attack. In this dribble, the ball is pushed low and quickly across the body.

Figure 3.16a–c Crossover dribble: *(a)* low dribble (one hand), *(b)* crossover low and in front of body, and *(c)* low dribble (opposite hand).

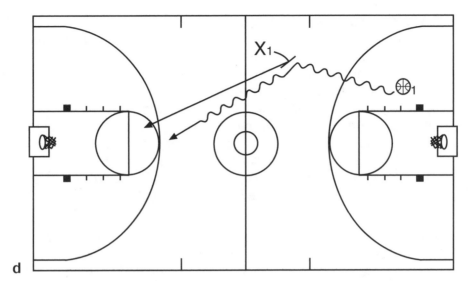

Figure 3.16d Crossover dribble right to left; offensive zigzag pushing off right foot, stepping with left as ball is crossed over (low and quick) from right hand to left hand.

The proper technique is to push the ball from right to left (or vice versa) as a zigzag move or V-cut from right to left (or vice versa) is made. This move is used when the defender overplays the path of the dribbler on the ball side. Teach players to make the move before a defender gets too close and to explode past the defender as the move is made.

Head-and-Shoulders Move. The head-and-shoulders move is an advanced move. It is a dribble move to get around a defender using the preferred hand (figure 3.17).

Figure 3.17a–c Head-and-shoulders move: (*a*) weight on right foot, dribble ball on right side, (*b*) zigzag on left foot, head-and-shoulders fake to left, and (*c*) move past the defender with right foot.

The ball is dribbled with the preferred hand. Then the move is continued by a fake opposite with a zigzag move on the opposite foot as a head-and-shoulders fake is made to that side. The ball is kept in rhythm with that move. The move past the defender then is made with the preferred foot. The rhythm is right/left/right to step by (when dribbling on the right side of the body). The advantage of this faking move is that the dribbler can face and see the defense while executing a dribble move to get around a defender with the preferred hand. The sequence for a right-handed person is push from the right foot as the dribble is made; fake left with the foot, head, and shoulders; extend the right foot with a long step forward and past the defender as the ball is pushed out in front; and step with the left foot and go to the basket past the defender.

Head-and-Shoulders Crossover Move. A head-and-shoulders crossover is another advanced move. It is a dribble move to cross the ball over from the preferred hand to the other hand while the dribbler moves past the defender on that side while still facing the defense (figure 3.18). This move begins like the

Figure 3.18a–e Head-and-shoulders crossover: *(a)* weight on right foot, dribble ball on right side, *(b)* zigzag on left foot, *(c)* weight back to right foot, *(d)* cross ball over in front of body from right to left, and *(e)* explode to basket.

head-and-shoulders move. The crossover dribble is kept low and is made across the body at the same time the zigzag move is made from the preferred side to the other side. The footwork is right/left/right/left to cross over from right to left and reverse when going from left to right. The dribble rhythm is timed with the footwork movement. The move must be made before the defender is close enough to reach the crossover dribble when it is made. This is the companion to the head-and-shoulders move. The sequence for a right-handed person is foot, head, and shoulders left; come back right (short step); short step with the left foot as the ball is crossed over in front of the body from right to left; and bring the right foot across and go to the basket past the defender.

Spin Dribble.   A spin or whirl dribble is used for maximum ball protection when the ballhandler is closely guarded. During this move the body is kept between the ball and defender as shown in figure 3.19. The disadvantage of this

a   b

c   d

Figure 3.19a–d   Spin or whirl dribble: *(a)* low dribble, quick stop, *(b)* rear turn, *(c)* pull ball (keep it in the holster and tight to the hip), and *(d)* change hands and move past defender.

Critical Cue

Pull ball to hip
on the spin dribble.

Critical Cue

Move in, out, and by on
the back dribble move.

move is that the ballhandler loses sight of defenders and teammates briefly and may be susceptible to blind side traps or double teams. Spin dribble footwork uses a quick stop, rear-turn pivot, and sharp angled zigzag moves from right to left (or vice versa). As the 270° rear turn is made on the left (or right) foot the right (or left) hand pulls the ball with the pivot until the turn is completed and the first step is made with the right (or left) foot. The ball is kept close to the body—the pull is similar to pulling a pistol from a holster. Have players pull the ball and keep it tight near the hip/leg to avoid the defenders' reach- or slap-around moves. After the rear turn is completed, the ball is switched to the opposite hand and full-court vision is regained. This move changes direction from an angle that is forward right to forward left (or vice versa) as the ball is changed from the right hand to the left hand (or vice versa).

Back Dribble.   The rocker dribble or back dribble move is used to back away from trouble, defensive traffic, or a trap (figure 3.20). When dribbling with the right (left) hand, players should be in a control-dribble position with the left (right) foot forward into trouble, then explode back (out move) in a sliding movement to get away from the defense. After reestablishing a gap on the defense, any dribble move may be used to penetrate or go by the defender. The crossover dribble is especially effective following the dribble rocker. The move is into the defender, back out, then by the defender with a sharp angle move.

Figure 3.20a–b   Back dribble: (a) when in the trap use low dribble and (b) sliding steps backward to get out and go by the defender.

Behind-the-Back Dribble.   One of the most popular dribble moves is the behind-the-back dribble. It is used to change hands (usually from the preferred hand to the nonpreferred hand) and go past a defender who is overplaying on the right (left). This is done by changing direction slightly to the left (right) and going by on the dribbler's left (right). Plant the inside foot and step past the defender with the outside leg. As the left (right) foot is moved forward, the ball is moved from right to left (or vice versa) behind the back, coming up under the left (right) hand for a continuation of the dribble. The coordination of the dribble and footwork can be learned by a stationary position yo-yo V dribble (figure 3.21); players dribble with the one hand back and forth with the opposite foot forward. When the ball is controlled from front to back it can be moved behind the back as a step is taken with the left foot (figure 3.22).

Figure 3.21 Progression for behind-the-back dribble: stationary position for yo-yo V dribble.

Figure 3.22a–e Behind-the-back dribble—right-to-left hand move: *(a)* dribble with right hand, *(b)* move left foot forward, *(c and d)* move ball from right to left behind back, and *(e)* continue dribble with left hand, moving past defender.

Critical Cue

One-foot quick stop and snap the ball on the between-the-legs dribble.

Between-the-Legs Dribble. The between-the-legs dribble is used to avoid overplay and to change the ball from one hand to the other. When the ball is being dribbled with the right hand, it can be changed to the left hand and between the legs when the left or right foot is forward (best with the right foot forward). This move is reversed for a left-hand dribble. The ball is kept low and crossed over between the legs with a quick, hard push across (snap ball between legs as you step with other foot) (figure 3.23). The coordination of the dribble and the footwork can be learned by walking forward slowly as the ball is crossed over between the legs during each step.

a　　　　　　　　　　b　　　　　　　　　　c

Figure 3.23a-c Between-the-legs dribble: *(a)* dribble with right hand, *(b)* push between the legs when one foot is forward, and *(c)* change to left hand.

The move is really a one-foot quick stop on the outside foot as the ball is snapped between the legs and a sharp angle step is made by the defender as the ball is switched to the other hand. The planted outside foot is then pulled past the defender to protect the ball. The between-the-legs dribble is preferred by the authors as the best dribble move to combat pressure, see the whole court, and move by a defender.

Coaching Points For Dribbling

- Keep your head up. See the net and the whole court.
- Control the ball with the fingers and the pads of the hands.
- Massage the ball and dribble firmly.
- Use a quick stop and chin the ball when ending the dribble or pit and protect the ball and be ready to pass.
- Pass first, dribble last.

BASIC BALLHANDLING DRILLS

These drills involve "ball" skills and are usually enjoyed by players. Coaches need to be insistent upon quick and proper execution and timing for all ballhandling skills. Players tend to learn them at slow speed and then progress to moves at game speed.

Line Drill: Passing-Catching

PURPOSE

To teach passing-catching techniques and all basic passes (two-hand chest, one-hand push, overhead, and baseball).

EQUIPMENT

One ball per line and half-court floor space.

PROCEDURE

Players are in four lines behind the baseline at one end of the court with coach(es) at "top of key" distance from baseline, directing drill. The first player in each line starts at free throw line distance facing the baseline. Ball starts with player on baseline. Passes are made as the passer quickly moves to replace the catcher. Critical cues are: pass with feet on floor, catch with feet (slightly) in air, passers exaggerate follow-through, pass with a ping, pass to a spot, catchers give a target, catch ball with eyes and both hands, play two-handed basketball. Properly first—quickly second. Suggested progressions are

- chest pass:
  air, bounce
- push pass:
  right side (air, bounce)
  left side (air, bounce); go pit to pit quickly
  read the defense (fake high and pass low or fake low and pass high)
  passer passes and assumes defensive position (designated hand position)
- overhead pass:
  catch, pit and protect the ball, then ball up
- baseball pass:
  face sideline and step with pass (move to "top of key" distance)
  fake pass into hand and then pass.

Two-Player Passing-Catching Drill

PURPOSE

To teach passing-catching using a push pass with either hand, after a dribble.

EQUIPMENT

One ball per pair and full-court floor space.

PROCEDURE

Players are in four lines behind the baseline at one end of the court with all players in the inside lines with a ball. Player "pits" the ball, executes a dribble drive with the hand opposite partner who moves parallel to dribbler. Dribbler quick stops and push passes to partner with the hand closest to him/her. Partner catches ball with feet in air and repeats dribble drive cycle. Catcher calls passer's name before pass is made. Complete sequence is shown in figure 3.24. The next pair begins their pass-catch sequence when the previous pair is 15–18 feet ahead (FT line).

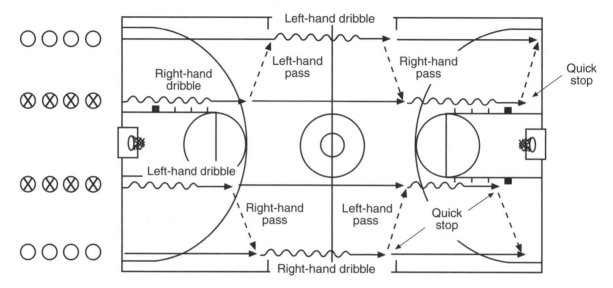

Figure 3.24 Two-player pass-catch.

Two-on-One Passing Drill

PURPOSE

Teach passing-catching between partners who must pass by a defender.

EQUIPMENT

One ball per three players and floor space of 15–20 feet.

Critical Cue

Pass with feet on floor, take ball to defender, use vertical fakes, be quick and accurate, catch with feet in air, and watch 15-18 foot spacing.

PROCEDURE

Players are grouped in threes; two offensive players 15–18 feet apart, with a defender between as shown in figure 3.25. Defensive players rotate out each 30 seconds or when an interception is made.

The recommended progression would be

- defender in position, designated hand position (up, down);
- defender close to passer, or away from passer (teaches passer to take the ball to the defender to take away reaction time [see O_5, O_6]); and
- live defense and offense.

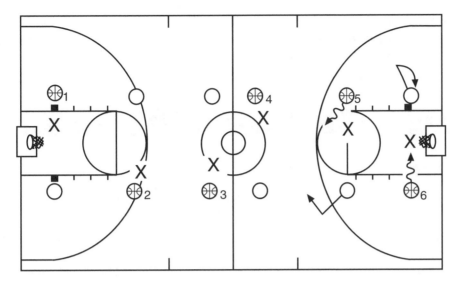

Figure 3.25 Two-on-one passing.

Moving Pairs Passing

PURPOSE

To teach partner passing and catching skills while moving and when playing against a defender.

EQUIPMENT

One ball and floor space of 15–18 feet in diameter per pair of players

PROCEDURE

Organize pairs of players with a ball and a court area—one passer and one receiver. The receiver gets open, receives the pass with feet in the air, quick stops, catches the ball, and faces the passer in a triple-threat position. The passer then becomes the next receiver. The drill involves continuous passing and catching (figure 3.26). All passing and catching rules

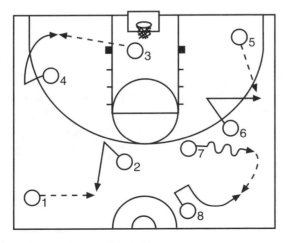

Figure 3.26 Moving pairs passing and catching.

are practiced. For example, pass with feet on the floor and catch with feet in the air. Another phase could be catch, dribble drive, quick stop, and pass. Catchers need to time their cut to get open just before the passer is ready to pass the ball.

Wall Passing

PURPOSE

To teach players the individual ballhandling skills of passing and catching without a teammate.

EQUIPMENT

One ball per player and a wall space or tossback rebounding device.

PROCEDURE

All basic passes can be practiced against a wall. A target also may be added. The Tossback, a commercial rebound device, has been found to be especially helpful for practicing this skill. It rewards a good pass by returning the ball on target and informs the athlete when an inaccurate pass is made. The following passes should be practiced: chest, bounce, overhead, baseball, and push. Remember to have players pass the ball with feet on the floor and catch the ball with feet in the air. This device can be used to gradually increase speed and intensity until a mistake is made.

Line Drill: Dribble, Pass, and Catch

PURPOSE

Teach players to combine dribbling, starting, stopping, passing, catching, and turning skills.

EQUIPMENT

One ball per line.

PROCEDURE

The first player in each line is in an offensive quick stance position with the ball (TT). On command, the player dribbles forward past the free throw line distance, quick stops, uses a rear turn on their permanent pivot foot (nondominant foot), faces the catcher on the baseline (next person) and makes a push pass to them and goes to the back of that line. The coach can designate any pass to be used.

Ballhandling Drills

PURPOSE

Teach players to control ball, become familiar with the ball—see it, hear it, feel it.

EQUIPMENT

One ball per player and six-foot circle of floor space.

PROCEDURE

Each player spreads out in his or her area and executes the following drill options shown—work for proper execution first and quickness second.

FIGURE EIGHT SPEED DRIBBLE

Start the drill with either the right or left hand, start dribbling in and out between your legs in a figure eight manner (figure 3.27a). Start slowly and keep the ball as low as possible at all times. Gradually pick up speed after you begin to master the drill. There is no time limit to the drill, although 20 times around in a minute is excellent, 10 in 30 seconds.

Figure 3.27a Figure eight speed dribble.

BLURR

Start the drill with the legs about shoulder-width apart. One hand will be on the ball in front of the legs, as shown (figure 3.27b). Then flip the ball in the air and reverse the position of your hands. Catch the ball in the fingertips and try to go as fast as you can for 30 seconds. The ball will seem to sit between your legs if executed properly. Excellent—80–100; Good—60–80; Fair—40–60.

Figure 3.27b Blurr.

STRADDLE FLIP

Start with the legs shoulder-width apart with the knees bent and the hands in front holding the basketball. Let go of the ball or flip it very slightly up in the air between your legs. Now bring your hands to the back of your legs and catch the ball before it hits the ground. Now flip the ball again in the air and bring your hands back to the front as quickly as you can (figure 3.27c). Drill as fast as you can without dropping the ball. Drill is done for 30 seconds. Excellent—90+; Good—60–80; Fair—40–60.

Figure 3.27c Straddle flip.

RHYTHM

Take the ball around the right leg. Grab the ball with the left hand in front, right hand in back. Drop the ball. Quickly reverse hands and catch the ball after one bounce. Move the ball back to start around left leg. Opposite drill is to start with the ball in the left hand (figure 3.27d). Drill is done for 30 seconds. Excellent—33–40; Good—21–32; Fair—10–20.

Figure 3.27d Rhythm.

DOUBLE LEG/SINGLE LEG

Take the ball behind the legs and around to the front. When the ball reaches the right hand, spread your legs and take the ball around the right leg only. Then close your legs and take the ball once around both legs, then open your legs and take the ball around your left leg once then back to two legs again. The ball always moves in the same direction (figure 3.27e). Opposite drill is to start the ball in the left hand. Drill is done for 30 seconds. Excellent—50–70; Good—35–50; Fair—25–35.

Figure 3.27e Double leg/single leg.

AROUND THE WAIST

Take the ball in the right hand and move it behind your back and catch it with your left hand and in one continuous motion bring the ball around to the front to your right hand. Do the drill continuously for 30 seconds, as fast as possible. Drill is then done by starting with the ball in the left hand (figure 3.27f). Excellent—55–70; Good—35–50; Fair—25–35.

Figure 3.27f Around the waist.

AROUND THE HEAD

Place the ball in the right hand, and with your shoulders back, take the ball behind your head and catch it with your left hand and bring it around to the front to your right hand, in a continuous motion (figure 3.27g). Opposite drill is to start with the ball in the left hand. Drill is done for 30 seconds. Excellent—55–75; Good—40–50; Fair—30–40.

Figure 3.27g Around the head.

FIGURE EIGHT FROM THE BACK

Start with the ball in the right hand. Take it between your legs to your left hand, then with the ball in the left hand take it behind your left leg and between your legs to your right hand (figure 3.27h). Opposite drill is figure eight from the front, which takes the ball right and left hand through the front of your legs. Continue the drill for 30 seconds. Excellent—75–85; Good—50–65; Fair—30–45.

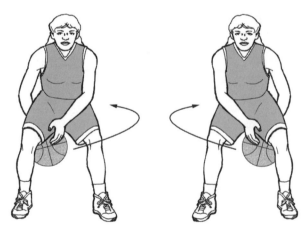

Figure 3.27h Figure eight from the back.

FIGURE EIGHT WITH ONE BOUNCE

Start with the legs shoulder width and the knees bent. With the ball in the right hand, bounce it between your legs and catch it with your left hand behind your legs, then with the ball in the left hand bring it around to the front and bounce it between your legs and catch it with your right hand (figure 3.27i). Opposite drill is to take the ball behind the legs and bounce it to the front right and left hand. Excellent—40–50; Good—30–40; Fair—20–30.

Figure 3.27i Figure eight with one bounce.

Full-Court Dribbling

PURPOSE

To teach ballhandling skills of dribbling.

EQUIPMENT

One ball per line (minimum) on a half court (minimum).

PROCEDURE

Using the line drill formation, four lines of players are formed on the baseline. The dribble moves of the drill are then practiced for one circuit. Players concentrate on maintaining eye contact with the basket at the opposite end of the court.

OPTIONS

• Speed dribble—players dribble down the court with one hand, then return dribbling with the other hand.

- Change-of-pace dribble—players alternate speed and control dribbles down the court, using the opposite hand on return.
- Back dribble and crossover (pullback crossover)—players dribble into an imaginary trap at the free throw line, half line, and opposite free throw line, and finish with a quick stop and ball chin at the end.
- Players use a specified dribble and must quick stop under control on coach's signal (whistle).
- Zigzag/crossover dribble or spin dribble—players dribble down court from a TT start in a zigzag, using V-cuts and crossover or spin dribbles.
- Two-ball dribbling (advanced)—players can dribble two balls while executing selected dribble moves (low, back, crossover, spin, etc.). Start dribbling hard and high, then low, then alternate rhythm (one high, one low). Then add changes of direction and speed and, finally, use different combinations.

4

Shooting

"The main thing is that we get a good shot
every time down the floor."

— from *Pete's Principles,* Pete Carril,
former Princeton coach, now Hall of Fame coach

Shooting is probably the best known fundamental skill—every player you coach is interested in scoring. If simply given a basket and a ball, even a novice invariably will dribble and shoot.

Shooting is a skill that can be practiced alone and one that produces immediate feedback. It is the fundamental skill that players enjoy and practice most. Most coaches contend that all players can become good shooters, because good shooters are made only through long hours, days, and eventually years of practice. It also should be recognized that great shooters also must possess very special physical talents. Any player, however, can become a good shooter and an excellent free throw shooter.

One of the two basic objectives of basketball is getting a good shot in order to score a basket. The other objective is preventing an opponent from doing the same. This chapter contains guidelines for teaching players how to get a good shot on every attempt.

FIELD GOAL SHOOTING

It is important to teach each player to become a scorer, not just a shooter. Anyone can shoot, but considerable skill is required to score consistently in game situations. In order to maximize their shooting-to-scoring ratio, players must learn when to shoot and when to pass, their range, and from what spots on the court they can consistently make field goals. The recommended minimal percentage guidelines for all players are shown in table 4.1.

Practice goals should be set at higher levels than game goals because of expected slippage in game shooting percentages that takes place during competition.

Shooting percentages provide a "bottom line" feedback measure of shooting effectiveness. Pay attention to practice and game percentages; beginners should completely adopt these shooting guidelines. If you are shooting below the desired field goal shooting percentages for your age group, you also should be receptive to adopting all the guidelines. Adopt one new idea if you shoot near or above the shooting percentage goals. Players always should use per-

Table 4.1
Desired baseline field goal percentages

Grade Level	PRACTICE % 2-pt.	PRACTICE % 3-pt.	GAME % 2-pt.	GAME % 3-pt.
Elementary	35	n/a	30	n/a
Junior High School	40	n/a	35	n/a
Senior High School	45	35	40	30
College	50	40	45	35
Professional	55	45	50	40

centages as self-feedback on practice and game shooting habits in order to assess status and progress.

It is important for players to develop a proper shooting attitude. This consists of concentrating on each shot attempt by focusing on the target and visualizing the perfect shot every time. They must learn to ignore distractions and see only the ball and the net in their minds. It is also necessary to build confidence over a period of time—this can be aided by players developing positive self-talk. Self-feedback is provided on each shot—successful shots are remembered and reinforced while missed shots are analyzed and forgotten. For example, comments such as "great shot" on a make or "off balance to the left" on a miss might be appropriate self-talk on shot attempts. Players should never be too hard on themselves for a missed shot—it is more productive to evaluate the error and then forget it: analyze and forget. Learn to play through mistakes.

Practice can make a shooter into a scorer—this is the secret of good shooting. Have players spend ample time shooting with proper form. Practice makes permanent (not perfect); therefore players must learn to practice game shots at game spots at game speed. It is also helpful to use mental practice—have them regularly spend three to five minutes visualizing successful shooting situations and specific shots. Imagine the look, feel, and sound of a perfect shot.

Proper shooting technique can be developed only if basic skills and strength are sufficient. Use a smaller ball and lower basket for teaching shooting skills before grade 7 (ages 11-12). Proper mechanics can be learned early, in grades 4 through 6 (ages 9-11), and readily transferred to a regulation ball and basket.

Passing-catching and quick stops are the most important shooting fundamentals. Players should learn to get a shot by first moving to get open (use proper footwork). Then they must catch and face in triple-threat (TT) position and be prepared to shoot.

Teach players to attack and get shots as close to the basket as possible on a dribble drive. They should challenge the defense by probing for the basket—the ultimate shot is the lay-up.

Acronyms can be used to assist players in learning some of the key concepts of shooting; two of these acronyms are BEEF and ROBOT.

Younger players can learn to shoot using the BEEF principle. This easily remembered acronym is a reminder of these shooting mechanics:

B—balance, the shot starts on the floor before you catch the ball with proper footwork—get your knees bent and feet ready first;

E—eyes, to be accurate you must pick up the target early and have a narrow focus on the spot target (imaginary center of rim or back of the rim or upper corner of backboard rectangle);

E—elbow, keep all arm motion in a vertical plane, especially keep the elbow up and in under the ball; and

F—follow-through, full extension of arm (lock elbow), hold for one count on a field goal and until ball goes through net for a freethrow. The wrist is fully extended with fingers pointed down (put hand in the cookie jar or make a firm but floating parachute with your hand). The proper release angle is 60° above horizontal. Finish high.

Critical Cue

Game shots at game spots at game speed.

Coaching Points for General Shooting

- Shot starts on the floor; feet ready first, knees bent.
- Balance and quickness are a key.
- Develop rhythm; get in a groove, feel the smoothness.
- Follow through on each shot (one-count field goal, net free throw).
- Quickness without hurrying. Be quick preparing for the shot, but don't hurry the shot.
- Vertical alignment; keep the ball in line with the elbow in. Young players need to use a two-hand pickup to get the ball up and to the shooting pocket.
- Use physical and mental practice.
- Use the BEEF principle.
- Become a shooting ROBOT.
- Take game shots at game spots at game speed.

Players should strive eventually to become shooting ROBOTs—scoring machines. A good shot means these things:

R—a player is in effective scoring **r**ange (practice goals of over 50 percent for two-point field goals and over 33 percent for three-point field goals;

O—a good shot requires that the shooter be **o**pen (no hand is in your face);

B—a good shot is always taken on **b**alance. The shot starts from the floor, so get the feet ready;

O—good shots are **o**ne-count shots where a player's feet are ready and the ball is shot in a single positive motion to the basket from the shooting pocket (no ball dip or swinging a leg); and

T—no **t**eammate has a better shot. Go up to shoot; pass if a teammate has a better shot.

Shooting Lay-Ups

All players should learn to shoot both left- and right-handed lay-ups. The technique is to jump from the left leg when shooting right-handed and vice versa when shooting left-handed. A high jump is made by "stamping" on the last step to minimize the forward long jump. Have players use the backboard whenever possible; exceptions may be the baseline dribble drive and the dunk shot. The dunk shot should be used only when a player can dunk the ball without strain and there is minimal defensive traffic.

The Approach.   Attacking or accelerating to the basket is a positive approach that your players can use readily. When shooting a lay-up, the attack move is made by taking the ball up with two hands (bring the free hand to the ball when dribbling, chin, and keep the ball chest high on the side away from the defender). Use a two-hand pickup to pit and protect the ball away from the defender. Players should keep the ball away from the hip. The last dribble is timed with the

Critical Cue

Chin the ball away from the defense on lay-ups.

step on the inside foot when using a dribble-drive move. Teach beginners to use a "gallop" move with a lay-up. For a right-handed dribbler and shooter the last one-two gallop move will be with the right foot and left foot jump, in that order.

The Jump. The knee is then raised high when jumping and straightened just before the peak of the jump (figure 4.1). Other tips for players include using the backboard to their advantage, shooting softly with a feather touch, and focusing on the ball and the target. The types of lay-ups to teach are the overhand or push (palm facing target—figure 4.2) and the underhand or scoop lay-up which produces a softer shot and is shot with palm up (figure 4.3).

Figure 4.1 Just before the peak of the jump.

Figure 4.2 Overhand or push lay-up.

Figure 4.3 Underhand or scoop lay-up.

Set and Jump Shot Mechanics

The movements for shooting the one-hand set shot and jump shot are the same. The essential difference between the two shots is that the jump shot is executed by shooting the set shot just before the peak of a jump. Proper shooting mechanics should be taught and practiced. The medium arc shot (about 60° at the angle of release) is the best compromise between the best arc for shooting (a trajectory that is almost vertical) and the available strength for accurate shooting. The shooting foot, elbow, wrist, and hand are all in the same vertical plane with the basket as the ball is brought up past the face (figure 4.4). As was stated earlier, the hand and arm motions are the same on all set or jump shots—the power comes from the legs. Backspin on the ball produced by the finger thrust increases the angle of rebound off the rim (i.e., it produces a more vertical bounce) and gives the shot a greater chance of going into the basket.

In addition to these general points of shooting mechanics, players should be taught specific fundamentals such as proper body position, holding the ball, and the different steps of executing the shot.

Figure 4.4 Vertical plane shooting.

SHOOTING MECHANICS

The specific movement techniques of shooting are called shooting mechanics. These include the mechanics of the body, feet, and hands.

Critical Cue

Get feet ready first with knees bent.

Balance

A good shot starts with the *feet ready (knees bent)* and the dominant foot slightly forward in a quick stance or offensive TT position. The head is balanced and slightly forward with the body generally facing the basket (the shoulders are not exactly square to basket—the dominant shoulder is slightly forward).

Target

When the ring of the rim is the target, focus on the imaginary center of the ring (the perfect target) or the middle eyelet on the back of the ring as you see through the net. For angled shots, use the upper corner of the backboard rectangle. Coaches should remind shooters to hit that target on the way down to have the same arch on ring and backboard shots (which tend to be shot too low or flat). The best court areas to shoot the "board shot" are shown in figure 4.5.

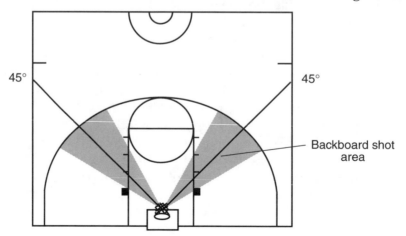

Figure 4.5 Use the backboard target at 45-degree angle.

The eyes should be kept on the target at all times. The only exception to this would be to follow the flight of the ball after release as a weekly drill to check proper backspin (described later).

Shooting Hand

The next step is for the shooter to grip the ball properly. The fingers of the shooting hand should be spread comfortably with the ball touching the whole hand except the heel (figure 4.6). The angle between the thumb and first finger is about 70°. This is done by placing the ball in the shooting hand while holding the palm up in front of the body (figure 4.7). When handling the ball, players can move it to shooting position by grasping the ball with both hands on the side and then rotating the ball so the shooting hand is behind and under the ball.

Critical Cue

Pick up the ball and see your spot target early.

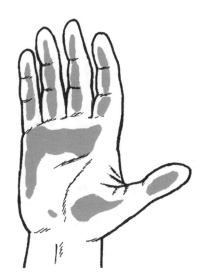

Figure 4.6 Shooting hand grip: use the whole hand, except for the heel.

Figure 4.7 Grip of shooting hand.

The next shooting hand technique is to place the shooting hand in the same position for each shot for consistency.

After moving the ball into shooting position, the shooter should bend the wrist back and lock it in (rotate it all the way in). Make an "L" at the wrist and at the elbow. (Set the ball on the hand and hold an imaginary tray with the shooting hand.) This position is illustrated in figure 4.8.

The elbow (the "L") is kept up, in, and in front of the wrist (figure 4.9). Beginners may have a lower starting elbow position, but the elbow should still be in front of the wrist and above the shooting foot. Younger players tend to drop the ball too low to gain momentum and in the process develop an inefficient shooting mechanic. The most common error with the shooting hand/arm is having the elbow out.

Balance Hand

The balance hand is used only to steady the ball, not to shoot it. It is kept on the side of the ball to avoid "thumb drag" and does not guide the ball. As the shot is released it is moved *slightly* out of the way. The balance hand finishes

Critical Cue

Balance hand is a guide, move it off the ball slightly before release, keep balance elbow bent. Point thumb up along with fingers in a vertical position.

Figure 4.8 Bend and lock wrist back (rotate in).

Figure 4.9 Elbow up, in, and in front of wrist.

in a vertical position off the ball and with the fingertips at the level of the wrist of the shooting hand. The elbow remains flexed slightly. Common errors of the balance hand are the thumb push (to shoot the ball), the heel push (to hold under and drag the ball), and rotating the off hand with the shot (it should be a stationary guide). These errors can be caused by extending the elbow during the shot. Figure 4.10 shows the correct shooting pocket position.

Release

Shooting up and over requires thrusting the fingers up and forward through the ball or snapping the wrist. Players should visualize shooting out of the top of a glass telephone booth or over a seven-foot defender. Backspin will be produced on the ball if the fingers *thrust* the ball up and over (snap the wrist) (figure 4.11). The ball comes off of the index and middle fingers last.

Backspin produces a soft shot that can hit the rim and bounce in. Check the backspin weekly by doing a vertical shot or following the flight of the ball after the release. Do *not* develop the habit of watching the ball—focus on the target.

The proper release angle is about 60° above horizontal. Most players' release angle is too low, which decreases the available target from above and lowers shooting percentage. Be sure to release high.

Critical Cue

Release the ball high, up, and over at 60° with backspin.

Follow-Through

The final step in shooting is to follow through with complete elbow extension (lock the elbow), arm pronation or turnout, and wrist flexion (controlled relaxation). Use the wrist for strength. Players should visualize putting the fingers in a cookie jar, putting a hand in the basket, or making a parachute with the floating hand and holding it (figure 4.12). The hand is firm but relaxed.

Figure 4.10 Triple-threat ball and shooting pocket position—balance hand on the side.

Figure 4.11 Thrust up and over—check backspin by shooting a vertical shot.

Figure 4.12 Follow through with complete extension and pronation of arm.

The Three-Point Shot

Shooting the three-point shot requires some adjustment. Three-point shooters must develop their sense of where the line is without looking down. Long shots will produce long rebounds and rebounding teammates must adjust accordingly. Knowing the time and score in a game is important for all shots but especially the three-point shot ("trey"). This shot should only be attempted as the player is moving toward the line with a quick stop or after a plant and pivot (figure 4.13). These movements will provide the greater force needed for this shot and allow beginning players to take it without straining. Emphasis should be placed on getting momentum from bending the knees more for extra power from the legs, using the elbow L, and on releasing the shot on the way up with full follow-through. For most players, it is more of a set shot.

Homer Drew of Valparaiso University teaches his players to get the three-point field goal shot from the pass in six ways, including

- inside-out passes,
- offensive rebound—pass out,
- penetrate and pass,
- fast-break to the trey,

Critical Cue

To shoot the trey, get momentum from legs, greater elbow range, and full follow-through. Keep the elbow in line.

- skip pass (with or without a screen), and
- screen and fade/flare.

Post Hook Shot Principles

This shot is used by players who receive the ball in a low post position with their backs to the basket. The best location for a post shot is just outside the free throw lane near the block (figure 4.14). This low-medium post position is taken just outside the lane near the first or second free throw lane spaces. The post player locates on the "post line," a straight line between the passer and the basket.

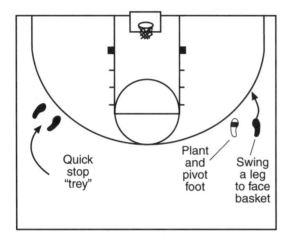

Figure 4.13　Footwork for the three-point field goal.

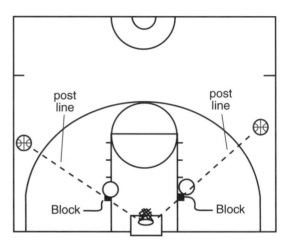

Figure 4.14　Posting up on the blocks.

The offensive player in the low post area should have the ball under the chin (chin-it). Any player receiving a pass should be in quick stance chinning the ball. The footwork for the post shot involves making a rear-turn partial pivot into the lane using the baseline foot as the pivot foot. The other foot is used to step into the lane as far as possible in a balanced position facing the basket. Ideally, this foot is parallel to the baseline. When the non-pivot foot hits the floor, the pivot foot is raised as the knee is lifted high and rotated as in a normal lay-up. The ball then is moved from the chinning position past the side of the head, pushed overhead, and released with full arm extension (elbow locked) and pronation. This move is led by the inside elbow. The complete post shot sequence is illustrated in figure 4.15 and includes these essential steps:

- Catch ball with feet in air when possible.
- Chin the ball.
- Make a rear turn and step into the lane with the pivot foot parallel to the baseline.
- Move the ball up and over with full extension and pronation of the arm, and keep the ball close to the body until the release.
- Rotate and shoot the post shot.
- Land in quick stance and assume the shot will be missed.

Figure 4.15a–e The post shot: *(a)* meet and chin the ball—use the quick stop, *(b)* step into lane, foot parallel to baseline, *(c)* protect the ball, *(d)* take the ball up and over, *(e)* follow through, face the basket, and assume the shot will be missed, with hands up.

Coaching Points for Field Goal Shooting

- Have feet and hands ready.
- Start shots on the floor; emphasize balance and footwork.
- Practice rim and board shots.
- Practice game shots at game spots at game speed.
- Practice shooting from spots, the pass, and the dribble.

Post Jump Hook Shot

A variation of the post player hook shot is the "jump hook." It is a simpler shot that requires less skill, is easier to teach, and has a quicker release. All players can be taught this shot which can be used close to the basket and shot over taller defenders.

The first and simplest version of the shot is to "catch and turn" in the lane, (i.e., the pass to the post player is made in the free throw lane). As the pass is made, the post player catches the ball with both feet in the air and turns to see the basket as the non-shooting shoulder is "pointed" at the basket. The ball is chinned near the shooting shoulder. The jump hook is shot from a two-foot power jump and a release directly up from the shooting shoulder with a locked elbow and flexed wrist follow-through. The sequence is catch and turn, jump hook up and over, land in quick stance, and assume shot will be missed.

Shot Fakes

Being prepared to shoot by having the feet and hands ready (TT position/shooting pocket) allows the player with the ball to be quicker and more aggressive offensively. It also prepares you to use the complement of the shot, the shot fake.

Proper technique for the shot fake is to take the ball quickly from the "pit" or TT position vertically as vision is kept on the shooting target. The body stays in quick stance as a short, quick vertical fake is made upward with the ball (less than six inches). Give the fake time to work—don't rush into the drive.

Critical Cue

Shot fake—short, quick vertical fake with ball only—stay in your stance.

FREE THROW SHOOTING

Free throw shooting can be improved by acting on the following suggestions. Your team must practice free throws in proportion to their scoring importance in a game (approximately 20 percent). For practices evenly divided between defense and offense, this means that 10 percent of total practice time should be spent on free throws. In a two-hour practice session, this would be at least 10 minutes spent solely on free throw practice. Because free throw shooting is a skill that must be practiced constantly if it is to be maintained, set up a plan for players to practice free throw shooting in the off-season with the same time emphasis.

Game percentage goals as shown in table 4.2 should be set relative to age level. These measures tell you whether to adopt the guidelines completely or to adapt your shot.

Table 4.2 Desired free throw percentages		
	PRACTICE	**GAME**
Grade Level	%	%
Elementary	55	50
Junior High School	65	60
Senior High School	75	70
College	80	75
Professional	85	80

Practice standards should be 5 percent higher than game goals because of slippage in normal game performance.

Confidence

Develop confidence in free throw shooting with a gradual, long-term approach. Players need to groove the shot early in practice and during the season. This is done by having them shoot consecutive free throws and groove their technique. Teach them to concentrate on every shot using positive thoughts, such as making the opponents pay for every foul, thinking net (shots that hit only net), and seeing the net ripple as the ball goes through. A positive shooting attitude also is developed by praising successful shots and evaluating missed shots. The shooter blocks out all negative thoughts and uses only the positive ones. Confidence is developed from the basis of proper technique.

Elementary age players should use a smaller ball, lower baskets (eight feet), and a shorter free throw line (nine feet). Junior high school players should shoot from twelve feet at a basket set at a height of nine feet.

Free Throw Techniques

The key differences from field goal shooting are alignment (foot position), keeping the weight forward, focusing on the same specific target each shot, pausing at the bottom of the shot, and establishing a ritual.

The complete free throw technique is shown in figure 4.16.

Players should know how a good shot looks and feels and be able to shoot free throws with their eyes closed. A shot should be executed with controlled tension—not too relaxed or too tight.

• Align—the shooting foot, elbow, hand, and ball are aligned in a vertical plane with the basket. The alignment of the shooting foot should be in the same spot every time and pointed toward the basket or slightly to the left of a line perpendicular to the free throw line. Place the toe of the dominant/lead foot (right foot for right-handers and left foot for left-handers) in the exact center of the FT line. Hardwood courts have an indented "nail hole" at the center for measuring purposes. On other courts, mark that spot. Put the lead

Critical Cue

See and say net, control self-talk.

Figure 4.16a–c The free throw: *(a)* align and get down with weight forward, *(b)* pause at the bottom of the shot, *(c)* follow through.

foot near the center and point the trailing foot at the corner of the backboard on the same side (right foot, left corner and vice versa). Place the feet shoulder-width apart in a balanced, staggered stance.

• Grip—the ball is on the whole shooting hand, with the balance hand on the side or under ball. After your ritual, put your thumb on a groove and point your middle finger at the air hole.

• Wrist—free throw shooters should place the ball in the shooting pocket and make an L at the wrist, just as they would for a set shot.

• Elbow—keep the elbow in close to the body, up, and in front of the wrist. Make an L at the elbow.

• Weight forward—shooters should assume a modified triple-threat position with weight more over the front foot, hold the head steady, and keep the back straight.

• Aim—the focus should be on the center of the ring or the center eyelet at the back of the rim. A player should focus on the target and think "make the defense pay" for fouling you. The focus on the target should continue until the ball goes through the net.

• Pause—at the bottom of the shot the player should pause for an instant until physically and mentally calm and focused, but no longer. After the pause, all motion should be up and over toward the basket.

• Follow-through—full extension and pronation are keys to the follow-through. The shooter should come up off the floor—get power from the legs. The upper arm should be at 30–35° from the vertical on the follow-through. Release high and hold the follow-through until the ball hits the net. Put your hand in the basket. Come up and finish on your toes or jump slightly forward. Stay in the shot and stay forward with your hand in the basket.

• Ritual—a ritual should be developed for the complete shot. Help each player do the same thing the same way, every time. It is much easier to groove a pattern that is always the same. A deep breath just before the shot should always be part of the ritual. Be slow and deliberate with your ritual. Keep the ritual simple; it is sometimes best to eliminate dribbling from the ritual.

Critical Cue

Always the same—
see and say "net."

Coaching Points for Free Throw Shooting

- Keep it simple and consistent.
- Start in same spot—foot on nail hole in the floor.
- Start and keep weight forward, stay in the shot.
- Have a ritual: breathe, thumb in groove, middle finger on air hole.
- Focus on hole and net; see and say "net."
- Eyes on target.
- Pause at bottom.
- Release high and hold follow-through until the ball goes through the net (put hand in basket).
- Balance hand out of shot; come off the ball, elbow stays locked.

SHOOTING DRILLS

Coaches should be creative in developing shooting drills. They should be sequential and progressive plus include all the basics of shooting: footwork and balance drills without the ball, spot shots, shots from a pass, and shots from the dribble. Emphasize correct execution first, then "game shots at game spots at game speed."

Line Drill: Shooting Addition

PURPOSE

To teach shooting in a simulated game situation.

EQUIPMENT

Half court (minimum), four balls (minimum).

PROCEDURE

Form groups of players in the four lines on the baseline formation. This is a form shooting exercise without the ball or a defender (the ball is added later). Players should execute a quick stop in shooting position after jumping from the foot closest to the basket. Later, the drill may be done using a ball and an underhand spin pass or a dribble.

OPTIONS

- Straight line—shots are taken without a target at the free throw lines and half-court line with players focusing on the basket at the opposite end of the floor.

- Offensive zigzag—a shot is taken at the location of each change-of-direction spot. Most movement should be lateral to make it easier for players to select the foot closest to the basket.

- Straight line with shots called by the coach—players in groups of four begin on the command "go," next four players begin when there is 15 to 18 feet of space between them and the preceding group. Coach designates basket to side of court (intersection of sideline and half-court line may be used). Players move forward under control in basic position until coach gives the command "shot," and at that time each player on the court simulates catching a pass with a quick stop and a shot to an imaginary basket. On the command "go," all players continue up the court until the coach throws another imaginary pass. Players must be ready to shoot with balance and control at any time, shooting to the right going down, shooting to the left coming back.

- Line shots with the ball—the first four players start together and use proper technique to shoot three imaginary shots (free throw line, half-court line, opposite free throw line). Shoot at the opposite basket and shoot as if the basket is to the side. With the basket to the side, land facing the opposite basket straight ahead. Using the nondominant foot as the pivot foot, pivot and face to the left, shoot; or catch and turn in the air to face the side, shoot. Players can shoot from a pass to self (two-handed underhand spin pass with backspin thrown at the location of the intended shot). Then players can shoot from a dribble. The shot is taken with a high 60° arch slightly in front of the shot location—the follow-through is exaggerated and held until the ball hits the floor.

Field Goal Progression

PURPOSE

To progressively self-teach the skill of shooting with a drill that provides a player with feedback needed for improving shooting in all basketball situations.

EQUIPMENT

One ball per player (when possible), basket.

PROCEDURE

Each player will take a ball and review shooting by following this shooting progression. Three to five repetitions of each of the options are carried out each time.

OPTIONS

- Two-hand *ball slaps* develop the feel of having the ball in the whole hand. Place hands on side of ball, toss ball up slightly, and *slam* hands against ball as you catch it five times.

- *Form shots* are one-handed vertical shots without a target starting with the ball in the hand in palm-up position. Then rotate the ball into the shooting pocket with the balance hand off the ball and slightly to the side in a vertical position. Shoot with good thrust (for backspin) and hold the follow-through until the ball hits the floor. Snap wrist.

- *Close shots* are taken with a target (rim and backboard). Remind players to practice from the inside out, starting close to the basket, and gradually moving out. *All* shots are in the free-throw lane.

- *Circle shots* is a drill in which each player will move in a circle, carrying the ball with two hands chest high (pit and protect the ball), using proper quick-stop footwork while shooting at five spots inside the free throw lane as shown in figure 4.17. After five shots are taken moving clockwise, have each player shoot five shots moving counterclockwise. Shots taken at 45° are board shots (2, 4), while rim shots are taken at the 1, 3, and 5 spots. No dribbling is allowed—circle shots focus on having the feet in position and hands ready to handle the ball. Rotate the circle after every shot.

  When moving clockwise, the proper footwork is to hop from the "basket side" foot to land with the feet ready to shoot from a quick stop facing the basket with dominant foot forward and hands ready (ball in shooting pocket). Counter-clockwise motion is done hopping from the left foot, clockwise movement uses the hop from the right foot.

- Shooting *from a pass* involves players tossing a high, two-hand underhand pass to themselves in a desired spot and using proper footwork to land in triple threat facing the basket ready to shoot. Shots from a pass are preceded by the "pass pickups" footwork drill around the three-point field goal line (clockwise and counterclockwise). No shots are taken—the focus is on footwork (figure 4.18). On "pickups," the ball is snapped quickly into the shooting pocket from a two-hand pick or grab. When receiving a pass or upon completion of the dribble, it is critical to get the ball quickly into shooting position.

- Shooting *from the dribble*—from a triple-threat position 15 to 20 feet from the basket, a player makes a dribble-drive move to the left or right, makes

Critical Cue
Use field goal progression every time— five reps of slaps or slams, form shots, close shots, and circle shots. Shots from the pass and the dribble should be used each practice.

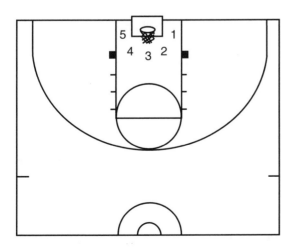

Figure 4.17 Circle shots: targets at five locations inside the lane.

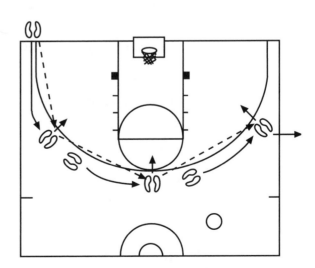

Figure 4.18 Pass/dribble pickups.

a quick stop, and shoots from a desired spot. Preliminary work should be done on pickup "technique." The footwork for shots from the pass and dribble is identical. With a dribble, the last *hard* dribble occurs as the basketside foot is used to hop into a quick stop facing the basket (lead foot forward). This can be done by having players throw the spin pass to themselves or having them take the last dribble with either hand, jumping from the opposite foot with a quick stop at the same time and landing in triple-threat position. Players go from baseline to baseline tracing the three-point arc using proper footwork and practicing the "pickup" technique (snap the ball into shooting position) prior to actually taking shots from the dribble.

Pairs or In-and-Out Shooting

PURPOSE

To teach shooting in a two-on-zero game simulation drill that covers all shooting situations.

EQUIPMENT

Basket and one ball per pair of players (players can also work in groups of three or four).

PROCEDURE

This continuous competitive-shooting drill, shown in figure 4.19, incorporates all principles of movement: passing and catching, shooting, and offensive rebounding. Players are grouped in pairs (there may be one or two pairs per basket). The basic rules are as follows:

- All pairs begin on the coach's command, starting with the passer under the basket with a ball; teammate gets open for shot, calls passer's name, and receives a pass for the shot.
- Shooters rebound their own shots until a basket is made (always assuming the shot will be missed), then gain possession to pass to teammate for a shot.
- Receiver must always get open and call passer's name.
- Passers make a quick, on-target pass at the right time to teammate for a good shot and go quickly to another location near the edge of his or her shooting range, ready to move only when teammate has scored and has possession of the ball.

OPTIONS

- Groove: each player gets open and shoots for 30 seconds while teammate rebounds; players take turns shooting and rebounding, changing every 30 seconds.
- Shooter makes five baskets and switches positions with teammate.
- The ten-scores game to ten made baskets involves players moving with shots from a pass and from a dribble.

- The coach designates the type of pass (push, overhead, air, bounce) and type of shot (regular or jab fake and shot).

- Pressuring the shooter involves the rebounder passing and making a poor defensive closeout while applying some type of false pressure (go by, shout, hand in face, contact) after the pass to the shooter. Defender cannot block or alter the shot or foul the shooter. At least once a week, use the variation of having defenders pressure shooters with hands up to help shooters develop the greater arch needed for shooting over defenders.

- Three-pass shooting involves shooting from an outlet pass (passer posts up), a pass to post (passer cuts), and a return pass for shot (figure 4.20).

- The *beat-the-star* variation places shooters in competition with a designated star shooter with a rebounder partner. Game begins with one free throw and continues with players shooting set or jump shots. Scoring rules for free throws give challengers 1 point for successful shots and 3 points for star on misses; challengers score 1 point for successful field goals and star gets 2 points for misses. The game can be played to 11 or 21 points.

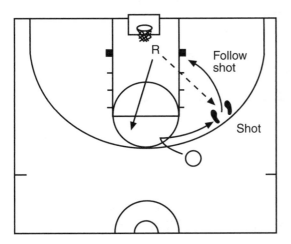

Figure 4.19 Pairs shooting: one pass.

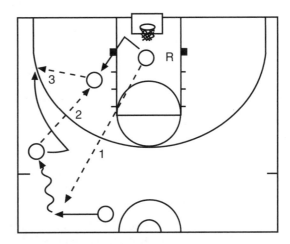

Figure 4.20 Pairs shooting: three passes.

"Make It-Take It" Row-Shooting Drill

PURPOSE

To teach the skill of shooting in a self-testing format adjusted to standards set by the coach.

EQUIPMENT

Basket and one ball per player.

PROCEDURE

All tasks in this drill are self-testing. They require the player to meet effective scoring standards. All moves are to be carried out consecutively without rest to practice shooting in game situations.

Players make dribble-drive lay-up moves (figure 4.21) from left and right corners (with foot on sideline), each hash mark, and the top of the key. They are allowed only one dribble and must make three baskets in a row from each spot. Front-court players with the ability to dunk the ball must do so by dribbling only once. The objective is to cover the greatest distance possible with a lay-up scoring move. After each row of three shots is made, the player earns the right to shoot free throws. The percentage goal must be met on free throws (4 of 5 for college players; 3 of 4 for high school; 2 of 3 for junior high) or the player repeats the move and free throw group.

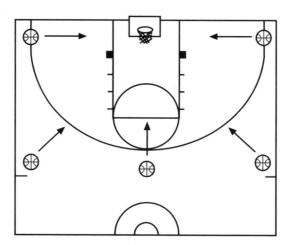

Figure 4.21   Dribble-drive starting spots.

ADVANCED OPTIONS

- Shoot from a spot with a selected move until you miss two shots in a row.
- Consecutive swish—shoot from a spot with a selected move as long you swish (ball hits net only) two shots in a row.
- Forty-point scoring—start three different scoring moves from five different spots along the three-point line: on the baseline on both sides, the wing on both sides, and the top of the key. First shot is a three-pointer from a spin pass. If you make it—three points. Second shot is a quick one-dribble pull-up jump shot worth two points. Your third shot is a drive after a shot fake and a power lay-up at the basket—worth two points. Finish with five free throws—worth one point each. A perfect score is 40 points; 7 points per 5 spots and 5 points per 5 free throws.
- Three-point contest—shoot five three-point shots from same five spots as the 40-point scoring drill. You get one point for every shot made, except fifth shot (two points). Perfect score is 30 points.

FoR BoBBY

Individual Groove the Shot Drill

PURPOSE

Teach a player to self-assess mechanics of the shooting hand and the balance hand while increasing shot range.

EQUIPMENT

Ball, basket, and teammate or coach to rebound and provide feedback.

PROCEDURE

Player shoots along a straight line directly in front of the basket moving toward the free throw line and half-court line. Start in close at about six feet in front of the basket and in the free throw lane. Place ball on the whole shooting hand (held horizontally facing up). Using only the shooting hand, rotate and move the ball to the shooting pocket (lock the wrist in and bend the wrist back—place the ball on the shooting tray or form the L). With the balance hand directly to the side of the ball (but not touching), shoot a high arching shot and hold the follow-through one full count. Continue moving away from the basket while using correct form.

This drill is a good check of vertical plane alignment of the shooting hand-elbow-shoulder (keep the ball straight) as well as using the legs for power. Keep the shot the same with the arms; get lower for power. The partner can help the shooter check position and mechanics. The balance hand should finish high. As the shooting elbow is locked and wrist is flexed for follow-through, the fingers of the balance hand are vertical at the lead of the shooting wrist.

Field Goal Correction Drill

PURPOSE

To focus on specific problem areas with shooters.

EQUIPMENT

Ball, basket, and coach.

PROCEDURE

Focus on one problem at a time: footwork, balance, shooting hand, balance hand, or follow-through. Practice from inside-out: 3 feet, 6 feet, 9 feet, and 15 feet from the basket. View the shooter from the side and from behind.

OPTIONS

- Footwork/handwork—have players move to right and left carrying the ball in shooting pocket and use a quick stop to shoot; then dribble right and left to shoot.

- Balance—check head/foot position before and after shot; head straight or toward basket (not left, right, or away)

- Shooting hand/balance hand—check shooting hand start (elbow in and L, wrist L) and finish (60° release, hold follow-through firm but relaxed). Check balance hand start (side of ball, vertical or right angle to backboard and floor) and finish (pull slightly off ball, elbow stays flexed, shooting hand above balance hand fully extended or balance hand fingertips at level of shooting wrist).

- Swish game (plus three, minus two)—count a swish shot as one point, a make that hits the rim is zero, and a miss is minus one. A score of plus three wins the game and a score of minus two loses; the winning and losing scores can be modified according to skill level.
- Consecutive swish—shoot until you fail to swish two shots in a row. Keep track of row swishes.
- Shoot until you miss two or three in a row and record the number of field goals made.

Foul Shot Golf

PURPOSE

Shoot free throws with competition against self or others.

EQUIPMENT

Ball and basket.

PROCEDURE

Start at foul line and play 18 holes. A birdie (one point) is earned for each swish. On a made shot (zero points), a par is made. If the foul shot is missed, a bogie (minus one) is assessed.

Players get three shots at a time or a round of three holes until all have taken a round. The game is over after six rounds. The player with the highest score wins.

Knockout Shooting

PURPOSE

Practice shooting in a competitive situation.

EQUIPMENT

Two balls and three to eight players per basket.

PROCEDURE

Form one line at selected distance and spot. First player shoots and rebounds own shot and, if made, passes back to next person in front of line without a ball. If missed, follow and rebound shot. If next shooter makes the shot before you do, you are "knocked out" to run a lap, sprint to opposite wall and back, or some other penalty before returning to game. Play for one- to three-minute periods. Coach can also play game with permanent knockout until a final winner is determined.

5

Outside Moves: Playing the Perimeter

"Drive and dish, pass and catch, and create scoring chances
for teammates is the definition of a point guard"

—Jerry V. Krause

Any discussion of individual offensive moves should begin with the reminder that basketball is first and foremost a team sport. So while every game situation will provide opportunities for individuals to use offensive moves while they have the ball, the player with the ball must closely coordinate offensive moves with four other players. As coach, you will need to place certain limitations on individual offensive moves to ensure players use their strengths.

Outside moves are, of course, offensive moves around the perimeter of the court. The four types of individual outside moves are

- live ball moves (when the offensive player with the ball still has a dribble available),
- dribbling moves (when the offensive player is in the process of dribbling),
- dead ball moves (made at the completion of the dribble when a player has used the dribble and stopped in possession of the ball), and
- completion shots (shots taken after a dribble).

FUNDAMENTALS OF LIVE BALL MOVES

Critical Cue

Start live-ball moves from the triple-threat position.

All live ball moves begin from a basic position with the player in triple-threat position facing the basket. The preferred way to get into position is to catch the ball with the feet in the air and to land using a quick stop facing the basket; i.e., catch and turn in the air. The alternative is to catch and face, that is, to catch the ball with both hands, quick stop, and pivot in triple-threat position to face the basket. This should be done using the nondominant foot as the pivot foot (permanent pivot foot) whenever possible.

The player should always protect the ball and keep it close to the body (pit and protect the ball), using the body as a shield. The player provides this protection in triple-threat position (TT) by keeping the ball near and under the shoulder during a live ball move (figure 5.1), by dribbling the ball on the side opposite the defender, by using a catch and face ("chinit" and pivot) technique in defensive traffic (figure 5.2), and by avoiding dangling the ball with elbows locked or extended.

Conserving time and space is a basic guideline for outside moves with the ball. All moves should be quick and made in a straight line toward the basket whenever possible. The offensive player should make slight shoulder contact with the defender while moving past on the dribble drive (figure 5.3) and use quick shot and pass fakes while maintaining a quick stance. The live ball move (using the dribble drive past a defender) should be made with a quick first step past the defender in a straight line toward the basket.

The attack-the-front-foot rule is applied when the defender is in a staggered stance (see figure 5.4). The most vulnerable side of the defender is the front-foot side, because the defender must pivot before angling back to cut off penetration by the offensive player. So the offensive player should be aware of the defender's front foot and use a live ball move to that side of the body whenever possible.

The player should attack the basket on the dribble drive by accelerating to the basket under control. "Now or never" means that the live ball move is best made immediately after the player receives a pass, before the defense can adjust, and while the defense is moving. If in doubt, the driver should pass the ball (pass first, dribble last).

Figure 5.1 Triple-threat position: side view and front view.

Figure 5.3 First step past the defender—brush the shoulder.

Figure 5.2 Catch and face—protect the ball.

The objective of any live ball move in the power zone is to score a lay-up with one dribble (seldom are more than two dribbles needed). Players should read the defense to anticipate chances to use a controlled dribble drive as a reaction to a defensive adjustment. Learning to control the dribble drive well enough to permit a last-second pass to an open teammate will help players challenge the defense even more. Pass and pitch or drive and dish are excellent perimeter moves.

Permanent Pivot Foot Moves

These moves should be used when a primary pivot foot is used for all live ball moves. The left foot should be used for right-handed players and vice versa. The moves that should be taught as basics are the direct drive, the hesitation move, the rocker stop, and the crossover step.

Direct Drive. This is a drive past the defender with the dominant foot. The right-handed player should drive past the defender's left side taking the first step with the right foot (and vice versa) by establishing triple-threat position in a staggered stance and pushing off the pivot foot. The quick move is taken with the free foot straight to the basket, as the ball is pushed to the floor and in front before the pivot foot is lifted. Finally, a step is taken past the defender with the permanent pivot foot to attack the basket. The breakdown count consists of the explosion step with the dominant foot (down), and pushing the ball ahead to the floor (go) on the dribble drive (figure 5.4). Playing rules require the ball to be out of the hand before the pivot foot is lifted.

a   b

Figure 5.4a–b Direct drive: *(a)* defender in staggered stance, *(b)* drive past defender on the front foot side (defender must pivot to cut off move).

Hesitation or Step-Step Move. This is a dominant-side move, made after a jab step to test the defender's reaction. It is done by establishing triple-threat position and making a short "jab" step at the defender and basket with the dominant foot. If the defender doesn't react to the jab step, a second "explosion" step can be made past the defender. The breakdown count consists of a jab step with a short pause (down), a long explosion step (go), and a dribble drive initiated by pushing the ball ahead to the floor (figure 5.5).

Rocker Step. Another dominant-side move is the rocker step: a direct-drive fake and return to triple-threat position, followed by a direct-drive move. The sequence is to establish triple-threat position, make a short jab step direct drive, then return to triple-threat position where a shot fake may be used. When the defender moves toward the offensive player in reaction to the return to triple-threat position, the offensive player should then make a direct-drive move. The breakdown count consists of: jab step (down), rock back to triple threat (up), explosion step (down), and dribble drive (go) started by pushing the ball ahead to the floor (figure 5.6).

a   b

Figure 5.5a–b Hesitation or step-step move: *(a)* short first step, and *(b)* long second step past defender.

a   b   c

Figure 5.6a–c Rocker step: *(a)* jab fake (down), *(b)* return to triple-threat position with shot fake (up), and *(c)* take long first step past defender reacting to shot fake (down).

Crossover Step. This is the basic countermove to the opposite side when the defender overplays the dominant side. It consists of establishing triple-threat position, making a short jab step toward the defender, and crossing the dominant foot over to the other side of and past the defender while keeping the ball close to the body and swinging it across at the same time. The ball then is pushed ahead to the floor to begin the dribble drive. The dominant foot is pointed toward the basket. Players should keep the pivot foot stationary while both the jab step and crossover step are made with the same foot. The breakdown count consists of making a short jab step, swinging the dominant foot over to the other side (long step) as the ball is snapped over from pit to pit, and pushing the ball ahead to the floor on the dribble drive (figure 5.7). The ball should be moved across the body (pit to pit) high in the chest area.

The direct-drive, hesitation, rocker-step, and crossover moves are the basic four live ball moves needed to combat most defenders. These moves are sufficient for most players. Beginners can usually depend on one basic "go to" move (direct drive) and one countermove (crossover).

a
b

Figure 5.7a–b Crossover drive for left-hander: *(a)* short first step (jab), and *(b)* crossover ball and free foot (move past defender).

Either Pivot Foot Moves: Advanced

These moves are taught when either foot is used as the pivot foot for live ball moves. Both right- and left-handed players should be able to establish a pivot foot with either foot when this method is chosen.

Direct Drive/Direction Foot. This move used to dribble drive past a defender consists of making the explosion step with the foot on the side the player is driving. The sequence is to make a quick stop facing the basket, and, when driving right, use the left foot for a pivot foot, and take an explosion step past the defender with the right foot. Also, when driving left, step with the left foot using the right foot as the pivot foot. The ball is pushed ahead on the floor on the dribble drive. The breakdown count consists of an explosion step with the foot on the same side as the dribble drive (right foot to the right side, left foot to left side), and pushing the ball ahead to the floor to start the dribble drive. Remember, the ball must be out of the hand before the pivot foot leaves the floor.

Direct Drive Opposite Foot. This move is used to drive past a defender on either side by using the opposite foot to step across and shielding the ball as a direct drive is made. The "opposite foot drive" is executed by making a quick stop facing the basket, and, when driving right, stepping past the defender with a left-foot explosion step and pushing the ball ahead on the dribble drive. The breakdown count consists of taking an explosion step past the defender with the foot opposite the side of the dribble drive, and pushing the ball ahead on the floor for the dribble drive (figure 5.8).

a   b

Figure 5.8a–b Either pivot foot live ball move—direct drive with opposite foot. *(a)* To the right with left foot, *(b)* to the left with right foot.

Crossover Drive. Players also should learn a countermove using either foot as the pivot foot (fake right, crossover left with the pivot foot; fake left, crossover right with the pivot foot). This is carried out by making a quick stop facing the basket, then making a jab step and crossover with the same foot to the opposite side (swinging the ball across and close to the body), and finally pushing the ball ahead to the floor and starting a dribble drive. The breakdown count consists of a jab step, a crossover step with the same foot while bringing the ball across the body, and a dribble drive started by pushing the ball ahead to the floor (figure 5.9).

Figure 5.9a–b Either pivot foot live ball move–crossover drive. *(a)* Crossing over from right to left (jab right), *(b)* crossover drive left past defender.

FUNDAMENTALS OF DRIBBLE MOVES

The dribble moves used following all live ball moves are described in detail in chapter 3—Ballhandling. Proficiency in live ball moves should be coupled with the development of quick, controlled dribble moves.

FUNDAMENTALS OF DEAD BALL MOVES

These maneuvers are used at the completion of a dribble move when the quick stop is made within 10 to 12 feet of the basket. They can be used when moving to either the left or right, but players must be within shooting range for them to be effective.

Players in possession of the ball should avoid dead ball situations whenever possible unless a pass or shot is anticipated. In other words, the live dribble should be maintained.

Either Pivot Foot Dead Ball Moves

These moves should be made after a quick stop: either from a pass or, more commonly, at the termination of the dribble. Remind players to "see the whole court" as the quick stop is made in order to "read the defense" and make a proper decision quickly.

Jump Shot.   Players should execute a quick stop and take the jump shot with balance and control (see chapter 4).

Shot Fake and Jump Shot.   Players should make a quick stop and follow with a believable shot fake (eyes on basket, short, quick vertical fake). The ball is moved head high while maintaining quick stance with legs locked for a jump shot.

Step-Through Move: Advanced.   The advanced move past either side of the defender to shoot a lay-up after a quick stop (with or without a shot fake) is another attacking option. Players should make a quick stop facing the basket, followed by a shot fake to get the defender out of quick stance unless the defender is already overcommitted. When going to the right, take a step past the defender with the left foot (or with the right foot when going left) and shoot a right- (or left-) handed running lay-up or post shot. The breakdown count consists of a shot fake, a step past the defender with the opposite foot, and a lay-up shot.

Crossover Step-Through Move: Advanced. This is an advanced countermove to step past a defender by faking one way and going the opposite way for a lay-up or post shot. It is done by making a quick stop facing the basket, then taking a jab step with either foot, a crossover step, and a move past the defender with the opposite foot to attempt a lay-up or post shot. The breakdown count consists of jab step, crossover move, and lay-up or post shot (figure 5.10).

Figure 5.10a–d Crossover Step-Through Move: (a) quick stop, (b) jab step toward defender with the left foot, c) crossover move (right pivot foot), (d) lay-up or post shot.

Spinner: Advanced.   A pivoting rear turn and lay-up or post shot is most effective from a dead ball quick stop at right angles to the baseline when stopped by a defender in the direct path. You can teach this advanced move by having a player make a quick stop facing the sideline and the free throw lane chinning the ball, making a rear turn on the pivot foot closest to the basket, and shooting a lay-up or post shot. The breakdown count consists of making a rear turn and stepping past the defender to the basket with the opposite foot, and shooting the lay-up or post shot (figure 5.11).

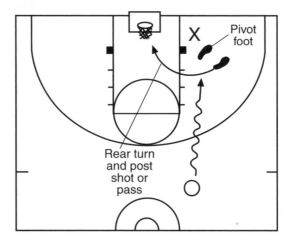

Figure 5.11   Spinner steps

FUNDAMENTALS OF COMPLETION SHOTS

All live ball moves and dribble moves should result in a pass, a dead ball move, or a completion shot. The completion shots to be developed are the basic lay-ups described in chapter 4—Shooting.

Coaching Points for Outside Moves

Train players to follow these general points:
- Visualize the defender.
- Use game moves at game speed.
- Develop quickness and balance.
- Go at top speed under control.
- Make legal moves.
- Execute correctly, then correctly and quickly. Do it right first.

PERIMETER DRILLS

These drills should be adapted to a coach's style of play and situations encountered by perimeter players in that style of play. As usual, they should be sequential and progressive.

Line Drill: Live Ball, Dead Ball, Completion-Move Addition

PURPOSE

To teach players live ball and dead ball moves and review dribble moves.

EQUIPMENT

One ball per line of players, full court.

PROCEDURE

Form four lines of players on the baseline. No defenders are placed on the court. Each circuit eventually should include a beginning live ball move, dribble move(s) in the middle of the court, and a dead ball or completion move at the far basket (figure 5.12).

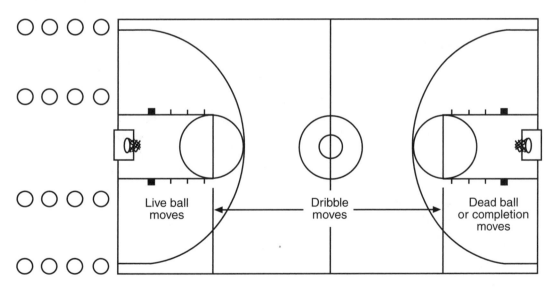

Figure 5.12 Line drill: individual outside moves.

There are two other line drill options. Put the first player in each line at the free throw line extended with the next player in TT position with a ball. Ballhandler passes to opposite player, closes out to play defense, and catcher makes a one-on-one move past the defender; dummy closeout first (overplay left, then right). Live closeout next if the one-on-one is not successful. The penetrator passes by the defender to opposite player and then becomes the closing out defender.

The second option is the first player in line uses a live ball move, quick stops at the free-throw line, and then does catch and face. Then that player makes a crisp one-hand push pass to the next player in the line. Finally, the passer becomes a closing out defender to the catcher who makes a live ball move around the defender. Repeat the action.

Spin Pass Outside Moves

PURPOSE

To develop skill in using outside moves.

EQUIPMENT

Basket and one ball per player.

PROCEDURE

Using a half-court area, a basketball, and a basket, have players practice live ball moves and completion or dead ball moves from a simulated pass-catching situation. Players use the two-hand underhand spin pass to themselves to begin the drill in all primary offensive locations and situations. The sequence is first to spin pass to self in spot locations near the edge of the three-point field goal line, catch the ball on the first bounce with feet in the air, and land facing the basket. Players should catch and face the basket every time they handle the ball by using the quick stop and the pivot, and then attack the basket. Set goals—two or three in a row with a move, make 3–5 baskets with a specified move, etc. Coaches should evaluate moves—remember that only perfect practice makes perfect. Either permanent pivot foot (basic) or either pivot foot (advanced) technique may be used for developing footwork. Using this self-monitored drill, it is possible to practice appropriate live ball, dribble, and dead ball or completion moves using the basic principles. A tossback training device may be used in conjunction with the spin pass technique to simulate passing and catching situations used with the outside moves.

OPTIONS

- Catch and shoot—spin pass to self and take a quick but unhurried, balanced shot.
- Catch and quick drive—spin pass to self, V-cut away, catch and face, dribble drive, and finish.
- Catch and one dribble pull-up jump shot.
- Catch, shot fake, and one dribble pull-up jump shot—quick, short shot fake with quick stance (legs locked).
- Catch, pass fake, and shoot—only move your arms and your head on the pass fake. Keep pass fake short and quick—stay balanced.

- Catch, pass fake, drive, and shoot.
- Catch, jab step, and shoot—create space for the shot—stay balanced and use a short jab step.
- Catch, jab step, drive, and shoot.
- Catch, one dribble, change direction, and shoot—attack basket on initial dribble, change direction (crossover spin, behind-the-back) to continue penetration and finish.

Closeout—One-on-One, Two-on-Two, Three-on-Three, Four-on-Four

PURPOSE

To practice all outside moves by perimeter players.

EQUIPMENT

One ball and one basket per group.

PROCEDURE

Form line of players under each basket off the court. The first player steps under the basket with the ball and will be the defender. A line of offensive players is placed 15–18 feet away facing the basket. The defender makes a crisp air pass (with feet on the floor) to the first player in the offensive line and then closes out to defend that player. The drill begins as soon as the pass is made for both offense and defense. The perimeter offensive player should catch the ball with feet in the air facing the basket, read and react to the defender's actions, and apply fundamentals to shoot or make an outside move.

Players may rotate to the back of the opposite line each time. Play make it-take it or any arrangement of their choice. The drill may be run as a two-on-two option (figure 5.13) that then becomes a teamwork competition with on-the-ball and off-the-ball play. Note the passer guards the ballhandler on the first pass.

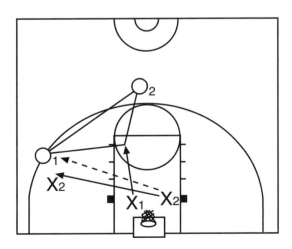

Figure 5.13 Two-on-two closeout.

One-on-One Drill

PURPOSE

To provide a variety of one-on-one competition for perimeter players.

EQUIPMENT

One ball and one basket per group.

PROCEDURE

One-on-one competition allows each offensive player the chance to evaluate perimeter play effectiveness in all situations: live ball, dribble, and completion moves.

ONE-ON-ONE STARTING 15–20 FEET FROM THE BASKET

- Have a two-dribble limit.
- Must begin with a "get open" move—V-cut or L-cut and catch-face.
- Make it-take it.
- Play games to five baskets.
- Use a five-second limit to make a move.

ONE-ON-ONE STARTING NEAR HALF COURT

- Use a cut to get open, then catch and face with ball.
- Use dribble moves to go by defender.
- Use a completion move to score; usually lay-up or jump shot.
- Can always use a teammate or coach for a passer.

ONE-ON-ONE "IN THE LANE" COMPLETION MOVES (DEFENDER ALLOWS PASS OR USE MANAGER WITH AIR DUMMY DEFENDER)

- Make a move from the perimeter and catch the ball facing the basket in the free throw lane.
- Score with a completion move (jump shot, step-through lay-up, crossover lay-up, spinner move).
- Alternate games to five or make it-take it.

ONE-ON-ONE FROM OFFENSIVE POSITIONS

Have the players receive the ball at the locations of the fast break or set offense.

Partner Penetrate and Pitch Drill

PURPOSE

Practice live ball moves and passing to a teammate for a score at the completion of a dribble drive.

EQUIPMENT

Two players, ball, and basket (can have three pairs per basket).

PROCEDURE

Partners start 20–25 feet from the basket spaced 15–18 feet apart; point-wing or guard-forward and forward-forward combinations.

The ballhandler starts with a live ball move into a dribble drive. The potential "catcher" partner times a cut to be open when the passer is ready to pass and with proper spacing. The guard-forward partners may use the cutting options of sliding away or filling behind into the driving path. The cutter may look for completion shots to the basket or outside shots—medium range or three-pointers. The penetrator/passer may pass (pitch) to the partner or fake the pass and shoot the shot. The forward-forward partners are on opposite sides of the floor. The penetrator drives the baseline and passes along the baseline using the baseline hand push pass to the partner-catcher who slides to an open position toward the baseline on the opposite side of the floor (baseline release).

6

Inside Moves: Playing the Post

"Get the ball inside first—take the ball inside
or to the baseline. Place pressure on the
defense to foul. Post play is a key to success."

— **Dean Smith, North Carolina, Hall of Fame coach**

Most coaches and players recognize the importance of establishing an inside game with a post player receiving a pass near or inside the free throw lane area. This inside game can serve several useful purposes. It can produce the high-percentage shot—the scoring opportunity close to the basket. The inside game also can increase opportunities for the three-point play—post players in a congested inside area are difficult to defend and are often fouled when attempting a shot. When the ball is passed to inside post players, the defense is forced to collapse in order to contain them. Passing the ball back outside to teammates can create outside shot opportunities.

The underlying concept in this chapter is an emphasis on another key element of the scoring objective—getting the ball inside for a higher-percentage shot and forcing the defensive team to respect the inside game in order to open up outside shooting opportunities, especially the three-point field goal.

POST PLAY FUNDAMENTALS

Post play is the key to building the offense from the inside out. Playing the post is a skill that requires a minimum of ballhandling and can be learned readily by players of all sizes with sufficient practice time and patience. Good post players get open for high-percentage shots by developing a variety of inside moves, considered "back-to-the-basket" scoring moves, usually from a low or medium post position (figure 6.1).

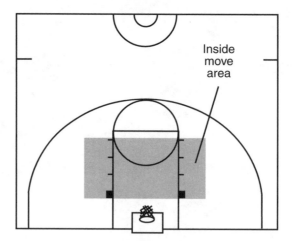

Figure 6.1 Inside move area—the low to medium post.

Penetrate

The offensive team must penetrate the perimeter of the defense on a regular basis by taking the ball inside using the dribble drive (penetrate and pitch) or the pass to a post player. The objective of offensive penetration is to create the opportunity for a shot taken as close to the basket as possible, usually inside the free throw lane.

Backboard Shots

Offensive players should use the backboard when shooting after most inside moves, especially when shooting from a 45° angle, using a power move, or in an offensive rebounding situation. The rule is "when going to the glass, use the glass" unless dunking the ball. Chapter 4 discusses the use of the backboard as a target.

Assume the Miss

Since inside players are stationed close to the basket, they can be primary rebounders. Because the shooter can best gauge the exact location and timing of the shot, a post player using an inside move always assumes the shot will be missed and prepares to rebound from a quick stance with the elbows out and the arms and hands extended above the shoulders.

Critical Cue

Assume a miss on every shot.

Everyone Is a Post

All players are post players. Though some of the best inside players have been medium- and large-sized people, technique is more important than size. A more critical factor is relative size—each player should be able to "post up" a defender of similar size or smaller and develop basic post moves. Cliff Hagan was a six-foot, four-inch center at Kentucky who was inducted into the Basketball Hall of Fame.

Expect Contact

Because the inside area is frequently congested, there is often considerable physical contact. Inside players should create contact and use their bodies to control defenders. Players must learn to initiate contact while maintaining balance and stance. Stay low with a wide base and feet active in quick stance.

Critical Cue

Get low and wide, create contact.

Hands Up

Passing to inside players is difficult and challenging, and there is little margin for error due to congestion and time constraints. Thus, inside players always should be prepared to receive a quick pass from a teammate by having both hands up (figure 6.2).

Patience

Many large post players are late developers and may have a poor self-image as a result of their size and relative lack of coordination. The prescription is coaching time, patience, and regular practice.

POST SKILLS

Get your players in a post player stance. The inside or post player must develop the ability to assume an exaggerated basic position with a wider than normal base, a low center of gravity, elbows out, forearms at 45° above horizontal, upper arms parallel to the floor as extensions of the shoulders, and the hands up and slightly forward with fingers spread and pointing to ceiling (figure 6.2). Post players should provide a two-hand target for passers. The hands are kept up and ready.

Figure 6.2 Post player's basic stance.

Posting up takes place on the post line (defined as the straight line through the ball and the basket). The inside player should attempt to get open just outside the free throw lane, near the post line. Establishing position on the post line shortens the distance the pass from the post feeder must travel. Ideally, the post player should be posted up with shoulders square (at right angles) to the line of deployment. This is called "showing your numbers" to the passer, i.e., they should be able to read your jersey number when passing to you. Keep the passing lane open by "showing your numbers."

Getting Open in the Post

The post player needs to get open on the passing lane between the passer and the defender whenever possible. This can be done by using a V-cut, stepping into the defender and using a rear turn to seal the defender, and stepping across the near leg of the defender (sit on defender's leg or fight the front foot). See figure 6.3. The offensive post player uses proper footwork to post up, then maintains contact and takes the post defender further in their set direction. That is, defender high—move them higher, defender low—move them lower, and defender behind—move them back.

Getting open at the right time is another primary task of the inside player. Because post play is a constant one-on-one battle, players must learn to *create contact* and stay open. Once the defender has taken a position, inside players should make contact to keep the defender in place. They should keep their feet active and use the whole body to work in a half-circle move (figure 6.4). Hips and buttocks are used to sit on the defender's legs and maintain contact.

Catching the Ball Inside

Post players must want the basketball. They need to build confidence in teammates that they will get open, catch the ball when it is passed to them, and score inside when open or pass outside when not.

Maintain contact in order to feel and seal the defender. The post player should be able to locate the defender by reading the pass. The passer feeding the post player should pass to the hand target away from the closest defender. The placement of the pass will help the post player locate the defender. Keeping the passing lane open is one of the toughest tasks to teach post players. Players must keep their feet active and maintain contact until the ball hits the receiver's hand; show your numbers to the passer (face them).

Post players must step into the pass and meet the ball and still hold their position. This is done by catching the ball with two hands, with both feet

Critical Cue

Catch and chinit in the post.

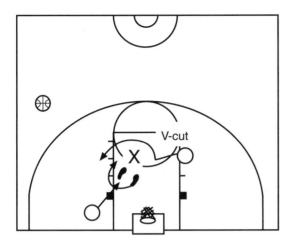

Figure 6.3 Getting open in the post.

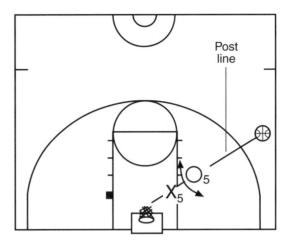

Figure 6.4 Half-circle move: keep open by saddling up on defender.

slightly in the air, and then executing a quick stop (except when fronted). Train players to focus on the ball until it hits their hands. When players catch a pass, they must protect the ball by using the chinit technique—elbows out, fingers up, ball under the chin. The lob or reverse can be used when post players are fronted. When the defender establishes a ball-defender-post position, two techniques are recommended. The first is an over-the-top lob pass (figure 6.5) where the passer shows the ball (go from TT to overhead), uses a check pass to read the help-side defensive coverage, and then quickly

Figure 6.5a–c Lob pass over the defender. *(a)* Both hands up—contact with rear end and hip, *(b)* use a check pass (pull the string) to test the help-side defender's reaction, *(c)* two-hand catch with power move.

throws a pass over the defender to the junction of the backboard and rim. The post player, maintaining quick stance and keeping both hands up (palms facing passer), faces the baseline and establishes contact with the defender using the hips and buttocks. The post player waits until the ball is overhead before releasing to catch the ball with two hands, palms facing the ball. The second technique is to use ball reversal to the high post or help side. If a defender is fronting on one side of the court, the ball may be reversed (second side) as the defender is sealed off and the post player steps to the ball (figure 6.6).

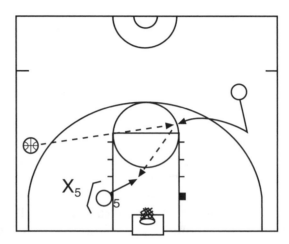

Figure 6.6   Post play: reverse the ball (second side), pin the post defender.

Taking Out the Defender

Inside players must learn to automatically take the defender out of the play. If post players are defended on the low side, then they should take defenders lower; if fronted, they should start closer to the ball and take defenders higher. If played behind, they should step into the lane before posting up with a V-cut or rear turn. The idea is to allow the defender to take a position of choice and then take the defender further in that direction and pin and seal them in that position (create contact).

Reading the Defense

When the defender is fronting—playing between the passer and the post player—have your players use a lob pass over the defender or reverse the ball, pin the defender, and feed the post from the opposite side. Offensive players should use a power move or reverse lay-up on the lob play. With the defender behind, a post player should catch and face using post facing moves. The post shot is also a possibility in this situation.

The defender positioned on the low side (baseline side) tells the post player to use the post or wheel move or the jump hook. Similarly, the power move or wheel move is indicated when the defender is positioned on the high side.

Reading and reacting for the post player means learning to feel contact, reading the pass, turning to the middle, seeing the whole court, and challenging the defense.

POST OR INSIDE MOVES

Finally, teach post players to move aggressively and be alert for open teammates. Their objective when using inside moves is to gain position for a close-in shot or to free a teammate in scoring position for a pass. This can be achieved best by mastering a few basic post moves they can execute well.

Post Shot

This is the move to the middle and into the free throw lane. It is the basic tool for the post player and an essential scoring weapon. The move normally is made without dribbling; the footwork and the mechanics of the post shot and the jump hook shot are explained in chapter 4—Shooting (Page 65).

Power Move

The power move usually is used to the baseline side when the defender is on the high side (away from the baseline). This move also may be used toward the middle when the defender is on the baseline side. The sequence for the baseline power move is to pivot with a rear turn on the foot closest to the defender and seal off the defensive player with the hips and buttocks. Then the post player takes one power or crab dribble between the legs, makes a two-foot power jump to the basket at the same time, and executes a quick stop with the feet at right angles to the baseline (belly baseline). This dribble sometimes can be eliminated when the post player is in the lane and close to the basket. Finally, the power move is used to protect the ball with the body and score with the shooting hand away from the defense; the backboard is used whenever possible (figure 6.7).

The power move to the middle is executed the same way: catch the ball and chinit (defender on baseline side), pivot on the baseline foot and use a rear turn seal, power crab dribble between the legs as a two-foot power jump to the basket and into the free throw lane is made, and finish with a power lay-up or jump hook (may need a shot fake). The most common error is to dribble/ drop the ball outside the base as the rear turn/drop step is made—this exposes the ball to defenders in the congested post area.

Jump Hook

The jump hook is a two-foot, hand away from the defender shot that is taken in close to the basket. The technique is to chin the ball and move the ball to the "pit" away from the defender. Then use a power jump (two feet) and use the arm bar to keep defender from the shot as the ball is taken up over the head and above the defender. The jump hook can be used with either hand.

Critical Cue

Power move—pivot, seal, power jump and power lay-up or jump hook.

Critical Cue

If you catch the ball in shooting range, make a quarter turn and use the jump hook. Point the non-shooting shoulder at the basket.

Figure 6.7a–d Power move: *(a)* catch and chinit, *(b)* rear turn and seal, *(c)* crab dribble—both hands, between legs, and *(d)* power shot.

Wheel Move: Advanced

This advanced move is a power move followed by a post move. The combination is used when the defender begins by playing high-side (or low-side) defense as the power move is made, but then anticipates well and cuts off the offensive player who has made a power move. The post player then immediately executes a counter post move (figure 6.8). The sequence is to initiate a power move, then quick stop and chin the ball when the defender overreacts and, finally, carry out a post move as a counter reaction to the defender's position.

a b c

Figure 6.8a–c *(a)* The wheel move can be made with the power move to the baseline, *(b)* post move back to the middle, and *(c)* take the post shot.

Facing Moves

These are basic perimeter moves used when the defender is playing behind the post player, especially with a defensive gap. The offensive player pivots with a front turn or with a rear turn on either foot. The front-turn options are the jump shot, jump shot with a shot fake, and the crossover post shot (figure 6.9). All live ball moves may be used in this situation. Other post player options are the rear turn on either pivot foot followed by a jump shot, the jump shot with a shot fake, or other live ball moves. This rear-turn move, first popularized by Jack Sikma, formerly of the Seattle Supersonics, tends to clear the defender and create a gap for the quick jump shot. See figure 6.10.

Passing to the Post

For most post players, the preferred pass into the post is the bounce pass, especially on the baseline side. The bounce pass is hard for the defender to deflect or steal. The air pass is quicker and should be used more often to the middle or on the reverse/second side pass and certainly on the lob pass (when defender fronts the low post). On the direct air pass to the post, pass from above the shoulders with an overhead pass and hit the post above the shoulders. Be sure you can see the numbers on a post player's jersey before you make the pass. This will ensure that the passing lane is open.

Figure 6.9a–d A facing move: *(a)* pivot on either foot, *(b)* jump shot fake, *(c)* crossover, and *(d)* post shot.

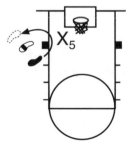

Figure 6.10 Sikma post move: rear turn (right pivot foot in illustration).

Coaching Points for Post Play

- Want the ball.
- Teach post players inside moves (one "go to" move and one counter move) they can perform with confidence and, in turn, have your team take the ball inside "in the paint" regularly so players can use these moves.
- Teach players to use the backboard on most inside shots.
- Consider all players who are competitive and who like contact as potential post players.
- Have post players keep hands up inside.
- Get players in quick stance with a two-hand target on the post line. Always catch the ball with two hands and chin the ball.
- Emphasize that getting open usually requires contact and quick, strong moves.
- Create contact to get open and pin and seal the defender.
- Take the defender in the direction they position themselves.
- Train post players to read the pass, their contact with the player guarding them, and the position of other defenders.
- Teach the post shot or the jump hook shot as the basic shot and a natural move to the middle of the free throw lane from chinit position.
- Show post players that keeping the body between the defender and the ball during the power move is essential to its effectiveness.
- Teach players the wheel move as a power move, quick stop, and post move in sequence.
- In some situations, a post player may catch and face to use perimeter moves, especially in the free-throw line/high post area or when the defender plays directly behind.

POST DRILLS

These drills should be developed progressively with no defense, dummy defense in different positions, managers defending with hand-held air dummies for contact, and finally with live defense.

Spin Pass Post Moves

PURPOSE

To teach players individual offensive post moves.

EQUIPMENT

Ball, basket, and optional tossback rebound device.

PROCEDURE

Post players use a two-hand toss and chin-it catch, an underhand spin pass to the floor and chinit catch (or pass and rebound from a tossback device) to themselves at a desired post location with their back to the basket. Players execute three repetitions of each post move on each side of the free throw lane. The inside or low post move sequence consists of the following elements:

- Post—to the middle
- Jump hook—around the lane (catch and turn, catch-crab dribble-shoot)
- Power—to the baseline, to the middle
- Wheel—to the baseline, to the middle (advanced)
- Face—jump shot, shot fake and jump shot, and crossover post move (front-turn option) or live ball move (rear-turn option)

No defender is used for this drill. The coach also may pass to the post to check post line, footwork, hand target, catching technique, chinning the ball, and post moves.

Post Progression Drill

PURPOSE

To provide players with a self-teaching progressive drill for offensive post moves.

EQUIPMENT

Ball, basket, and optional tossback device.

PROCEDURE

Post players begin with an underhand spin pass to themselves (or pass and rebound from a tossback) and make post moves in sequence. Five baskets are made for each move in the sequence:

- Power move—left side, low post
- Jump hook move—left side, low post
- Post move—left side, low post
- Wheel move—left side, middle/low post
- Facing move—left side, low post
- Facing move—high post, left elbow
- Same moves—right side

After players make the fifth basket for each move, two consecutive successful free throws are required for them to advance to the next move (or repeat the move again).

OPTIONS

- Require three post moves in a row and two or three free throws in a row.
- No defense, position defense, air dummy defense, and live defense progression.

Two-on-Two Feed the Post Drill

PURPOSE

To teach offensive and defensive post play skills, passing to post players, and movement after the pass for a possible return pass.

EQUIPMENT

Ball and basket, groups of four players (minimum) (figure 6.11).

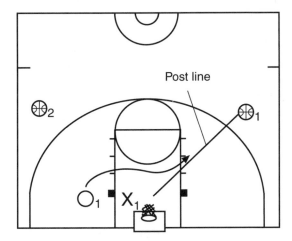

Figure 6.11 Two-on-two feed the post drill.

PROCEDURE

Two offensive and two defensive players work on post play from various locations around the free throw lane. All offensive and defensive post play principles are applied. Two players are needed as feeders. When defenders obtain possession, the first outlet pass or dribble for transition must be made. Have outside offensive players make a V-cut move for a possible return pass when they pass to post players and call the post's name.

OPTIONS

- Two perimeter players undefended plus one defensive and one offensive post player (rotate after each score).
- Two perimeter players and two post players; one offense, one defense. Start ball on perimeter at top of key. Perimeter player dribbles to either

wing and offensive post player gets open on that side—post may cut to high post or come outside and screen for teammate (pick and roll).

• Make it-take it two-on-two.

Mikan Drill

This drill is named after George Mikan, the Hall of Fame post player from DePaul who was the first dominant post player in history.

PURPOSE

Teach players footwork, ballhandling, and lay-up shooting close to the basket.

EQUIPMENT

Ball and basket per player.

PROCEDURE

Alternating lay-ups; shoot with left hand on left side and right hand on right side. Move feet quickly, be in a position to shoot as soon as you rebound and chin the ball. Catch the ball with two hands, try to swish each shot, and follow through each time. Never let the ball hit the floor—develop and maintain a rhythm.

OPTIONS

• One minute or three, four, or five in a row.
• Reverse lay-ups.
• Power moves—jump under the basket on the shot, catch and chin as you jump to other side, repeat.
• Power shot with shot fake (lock your legs on the shot fake).

This drill can be used for all players (perimeter and post).

Five-on-Five Post Passing Drill: Advanced

Developed by Mike Beitzel of Hanover College

PURPOSE

Teach post players to get open, catch ball, make post moves, and pass from the post position as they read and react to defenders (especially traps). Teach defensive players to double-team (trap) a post player and rotate to the ball on passes from the post.

EQUIPMENT

Ball, half-court space, and 10 players (5 offense, 5 defense).

PROCEDURE

Position three perimeter and two post players as seen in figure 6.12. In A, the defense allows the first pass (always) and the post player goes one-on-one (no traps). In B, a trap is made. After the first pass, all play is live.

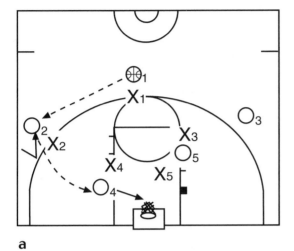

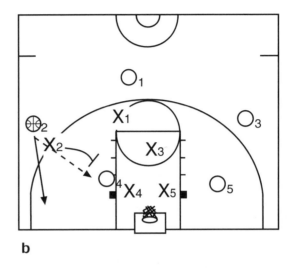

a   b

Figure 6.12a–b Five-on-five post passing: after each possession, the defensive team has a quick huddle, decides on a trap, and sprints to defense.

7

Defense

"My teams are built around tough defense,
stingy shot selection, and being hard-nosed."
—Don "Bear" Haskins, UTEP, Hall of Fame coach

Individual defense can be a great challenge for coaches and their players. It involves developing fundamental skills that depend less on ability than determination. In addition, defense can become a consistent part of each player's game. Both mental and physical challenges await your players in developing defensive skills.

There are basic individual defensive skills needed in all defensive systems: player-to-player, zone, or combination defenses. These essential skills are:

- defensive stance and steps;
- defense on the ball, off the ball, off to on the ball, on to off the ball; and
- special situation defense, screens, traps (double-team), and defensive charge.

It should be noted that these individual defensive skills need to be blended into a consistent defensive system. This will include level of coverage (full-court, three-quarter court, half-court), pressure/lane/sagging style, and assignments (player-to-player, zone, or combination). Individual skills in this chapter are oriented to an aggressive style of play; adapt them to your situation and team defensive philosophy.

Defense is a critical foundation to winning, tends to be more consistent than offense, and is more controllable. Ralph Miller, Hall of Fame coach, stated that losses are rooted in defensive breakdowns—individual or team defense, defensive rebounding, or turnovers caused by the opponent's defense. Defense also generates fast break offense, easy baskets, and offensive confidence.

FUNDAMENTALS OF DEFENSE

Defense is as much a mental as a physical skill. Players should be encouraged to be proactive, rather than reactive. Generally defenders are at a disadvantage to offensive players. One way to offset this edge is to use the rule that action is usually quicker than reaction. This can be done by emphasizing the active elements of defense represented as follows by the acronym ATTACK.

A—Attitude. The starting point of all defense is the determination to become an aggressive, intelligent defensive player. Each player must develop and maintain control of his or her playing attitude, especially on defense. Coaches cannot coach unless players decide to *play hard* during each defensive possession.

T—Teamwork. The collective effort of five defensive players is greater than five individual efforts. The synergy of defensive team chemistry can offset the natural advantage of offensive players; play together.

T—The Tools of defense. The four basic physical tools are the mind, body, feet, and eyes. The hands can be a help or a hindrance. When the other tools are used first, the hands can be a defensive plus.

A—Anticipation. Players must use basketball sense and judgment (mind) triggered by vision. They should see the ball at all times and use their eyes to anticipate. For example, you should see a careless pass instantly and decide to act quickly. Quickness is based upon physical readiness and mental anticipation.

C—Concentration. Players should be alert and ready to play defense at all times. They must assess the situation and be able to take away the opponents' strength. Players must avoid resting, physically or mentally, when playing defense.

K—Keep in stance. Defensive players must maintain defensive quick stance at all times. They should seldom gamble by making moves that take them out of position, and all players must be constantly ready to take advantage of opponents' mistakes. Keeping in stance is the most important concept for defenders. Coaches need to constantly remind players to "stay in your stance"—be ready.

Critical Cue

Stay in your stance.

ESSENTIALS OF DEFENSE

In addition to being proactive defenders, players must know nine essentials of defense: transition, purpose, pressure, position, prevention of penetration, moving, line of ball, blocking out, and communication.

Transition

The first task is to anticipate shifting from offense to defense. This requires an organized transition with communication among all five players and includes rebounding balance (assume shot will miss and get back or to the boards), sprint to protect the defensive basket, pick up the ball, find shooters, and recover to all open offensive players. Players going to defense should sprint toward the defensive end of the floor while seeing the ball (look over the inside shoulder), but may run or slide backward once the offense is contained. Defense starts when a shot is taken on offense and ends with a defensive rebound, steal, caused turnover, or opponent's basket.

Critical Cue

On a shot, go to defense or go to rebound.

Purpose

The purpose of defense is to prevent easy scores and to gain possession of the ball through rebounds or steals. Defenders must learn to prevent situations leading to easy baskets by opponents, i.e., prevent *all* lay-ups. Make the offense work to get all shots (and only under pressure).

Pressure

Offensive play has a basic rhythm that can be disrupted by pressure. Defensive play must maintain continuous physical and mental pressure on ballhandlers. Every shot also must be pressured physically and verbally. Bother players with the ball (live ball or dribbling), swarm the player with a dead ball (used dribble), and be ready to protect the basket and support the defender on the ball when defending off the ball. Pressure *all* shots. Ball pressure must be combined with off-ball position and readiness.

Position

Train players to stay in a stance when on defense. Most fouls occur when defenders are out of position or haven't maintained individual defensive stance. Get in and stay in a defensive quick stance.

Prevention of Penetration

Offensive players will attempt to take the ball toward the basket by passing or dribbling. Defenders must prevent this penetration. One defender always pressures the ball while the four other players play zone areas toward the basket to protect it and support the defender playing on the ball. Defenders should prevent middle-of-the-floor penetration toward the goal by offensive players using the dribble or direct air passes to this area when playing on-the-ball defense (especially the power zone shown in figure 7.1). Off-the-ball defense means keeping passes out of the middle of the floor (especially the power zone) by defending zone areas toward the basket area. Defenders should play zone defense and support the defender playing on the ball. Prevent the ball entering the power zone.

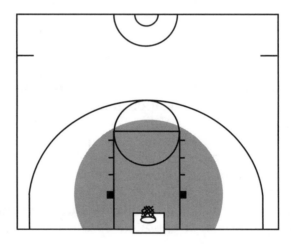

Figure 7.1   Power zone—located 15 to 18 feet from the basket.

Critical Cue

Defenders move when the ball moves.

Moving

Players must learn to move every time the ball is passed. All five players should adjust their floor position with every pass. On the ball, after the ballhandler passes the ball, the defender moves instantly toward the ball and basket. This is called jumping or exploding to the ball. When off the ball, defensive players adjust their position toward the ball with every pass.

Line of the Ball

The line of the ball principle states that players should defend their opponent only after they have taken a position ahead of the ball and toward their defensive basket. This is past the ball, a side-to-side line through the ballhandler's location. In figure 7.2, X_1 and X_2 need to get ahead of the ball at O_1 before getting in proper defensive position.

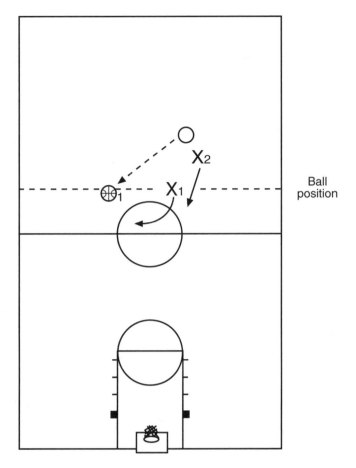

Figure 7.2 Line of the ball.

Blocking Out

Each defensive player is responsible for blocking (checking) offensive players from the basket area and gaining the defensive rebound when a shot is taken. Successful coaches recognize that defensive rebounding is an important part of team defense and devote appropriate time to teaching it.

Communication

Communication is always necessary for group success. All players must react to each other verbally and physically to produce an effective team defense. Essentially, the five players should act as one. Coach Mike Krzyzewski of Duke University tells his team that it is similar to the relation between your fingers and a fist. Fingers alone cannot accomplish nearly what they can do when gathered into a fist.

DEFENSE ON THE BALL

The player defending the opponent with the ball should get in and maintain a correct defensive stance. Defenders should be taught to maintain their position between the ballhandler and the basket (ball-defender-basket) as shown in figure 7.3. The head should be kept lower than that of the offensive player with the ball, usually level with the offensive player's chest.

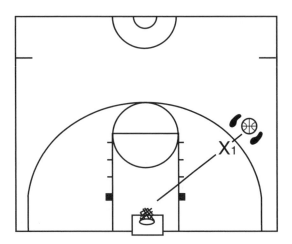

Figure 7.3 Ball–defender–basket: relative relationship of defender to basket and offensive player (with the ball) being guarded.

Guarding in a Live Ball Situation

Critical Cue

Ball-you-basket when defending on the ball.

One of the most common, important, and difficult tasks players will face on defense is defending a player who still has the option of dribbling. Once again, defenders must be ready in a defensive quick stance with the forward foot opposite the dominant hand of the offensive player. If that player is right-handed, defenders should have their left leg and arm forward to force the offensive player to pass or dribble with the weak hand. Have players defend with the palm of the lead hand up (see figure 7.4), which will allow them to move easily, flick at, and steal the ball.

Critical Cue

Hands on the ball and off the ballhandler.

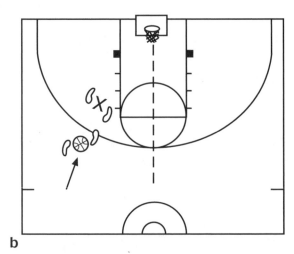

a   b

Figure 7.4a–b Live ball defense: lead hand palm up, trail hand palm facing. Left foot forward against right-handed offensive player. *(a)* Defensive stance, *(b)* foot position.

Generally, the recommended hand position for the lead hand is to keep it at ball level: ball low—hand low with palm up; ball in TT or high—hand high and palm facing ball. The lead hand is up unless ball is being dribbled outside scoring range. The trail or back hand should always be near the back shoulder of the defender and moving to cover that passing lane by the head (be a windshield wiper, or waving constantly). This puts more pressure on ballhandlers and increases the chances of their committing errors leading to turnovers. Some coaches always prefer to have the inside foot forward, as shown in figure 7.5.

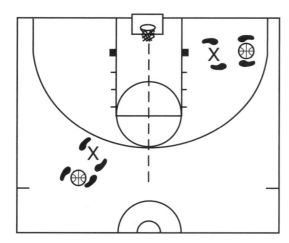

Figure 7.5 Foot position—inside foot forward.

Defenders play the ballhandler who has begun the dribble by cutting off the dribbler's path with the body and by maintaining ball-defender-basket position. The head should be in front of the dribbler with only the lead hand used to jab at the ball (when the dribbler goes to the defender's right, the left-hand lead is used and vice versa) as shown in figure 7.6. If the dribbler gets past the

a   b   c

Figure 7.6a–c *(a)* Defending to the right—point with left hand, *(b)* Defending to the left—point with right hand, *(c)* Ball flick—snake tongue.

defender, the defender should run to recover or sprint to reestablish basic position and the ball-defender-basket relationship.

Caution players that they must maintain space between themselves and the dribbler when the dribbler uses a spin, reverse, or whirl move. They should prevent penetration first, then pressure the ballhandler in a ball-defender-basket quick stance. In general, go low and stay low; don't hop and don't cross feet.

Guarding in a Dead Ball Situation

Critical Cue

Dead ball—
swarm or sag.

When a ballhandler has used the dribble, the two recommended techniques are swarming the ball and attacking the player's senses while staying in a stance as shown in figure 7.7 (pressure option), or dropping back toward the basket while staying in the ball-defender-basket relationship to anticipate the next pass and help the team defense (sagging option). The latter can be used especially when the ballhandler is out of shooting range.

Figure 7.7   Attack the senses.

DEFENSE OFF THE BALL

Critical Cue

Ball-you-player guarded
when defending off
the ball.

This is the most challenging and crucial individual defensive skill that makes a significant contribution to team defense. There is a natural tendency for players to relax away from the ball. However, they must overcome this and learn the importance of off-the-ball defense. Teach them that protecting the basket and supporting the defender playing on the ball is as important as attending to the assigned player away from the ball. These multiple tasks require greater attention than on-the-ball defense.

Off-the-ball stances will be one of two types: open (or pistols) stance further from the ball (two passes away) and a closed (or denial) stance closer to the ball (one pass away). These stances are shown in figure 7.8: X_2, X_3, and X_5 using a closed stance and X_4 using an open stance to support defender X_1 guarding the ballhandler. The common concept is that defenders off the ball are in a position of player guarded-you-ball.

There are several other guidelines to teach players about defending away from the ball. The farther the offensive player is from the ball, the farther the defender should be from the assigned opponent, always maintaining a ball-defender-player position. The defender needs to keep a gap (a distance cushion to provide extra reaction time), as shown in figures 7.8 and 7.9. In other words, the closer the ball is to the defender, the closer the defender should be to the assigned opponent away from the ball.

Critical Cue

Keep a gap on
the dribbler.

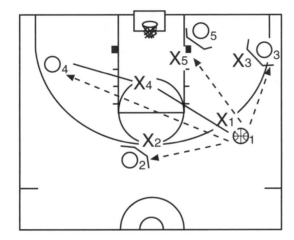

Figure 7.8 Closed stance (X_2, X_3, X_5)–open stance (X_4).

Figure 7.9 Open stance–off-ball defender forms the flat triangle.

What the defender does before the offensive player gets the ball determines what the player can do with the ball. Defenders should keep the ball away from the assigned opponent in favorite spots on the floor. It is a good rule always to take away an opponent's strength on or off the ball.

Player cuts to the ball (ball-defender-player position) in the middle or power zone areas should be prevented. Teach defenders to force offensive players to go around or away from a desired position. If contact must be made, the defender should beat the offensive player to a desired spot, make contact using an arm bar and a closed stance, and then reestablish a gap.

It will be easier to defend the ballhandler and support the defender playing on the ball if defenders see the ball at all times. Players should follow the ball visually to anticipate offensive cuts and careless passes.

Players two passes away from the ball should assume an open stance, which allows them to see the ball and their assigned opponent. In this position, one hand points at the ball and the other points at the opponent—a position termed *pointing your pistols*. This is also called forming a flat triangle: ball, you, player being guarded (figure 7.9).

Defenders near the ball need to develop the skill of denying the pass to the player they are guarding—this is called a closed stance. In a closed stance, you need to place your back partially to the ball (seeing both the ball over your shoulder and the player you are guarding) while putting the lead foot and lead hand in the passing lane, with the thumb down and palm facing the ball. Put your chin at the level of the offensive player's shoulder. Denial pressure can vary from hand in the passing lane (moderate) to elbow in lane and shoulder/head in the lane (high).

In a closed stance (denying the pass to player guarded), the offensive player will need to V-cut to get open, so the defender must stay in a closed stance and move continually to maintain the desired ball-you-player guarded position. Also, when overplayed, the player guarded may cut behind the defender in a "backdoor" move. The proper response to the backdoor cut is to go with and stay in the ball-you-player guarded closed stance position (snap the head and change the denial hand) until the cutter reaches the lane, then "open up" and assume the open stance to see the ball. Do not follow the cutter away from the ball. See figure 7.10.

Critical Cue

Closed stance—hand in lane, thumb down, chin on shoulder, positioned ball-you-player.

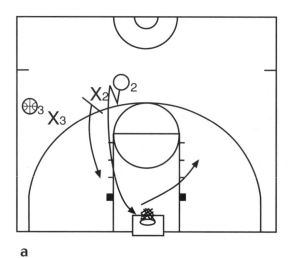
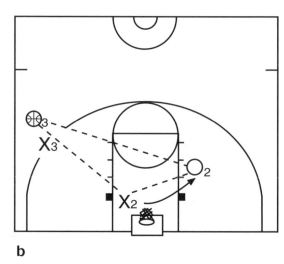

a   b

Figure 7.10 Defending the backdoor cut: *(a)* move with cutter, *(b)* open up away from ball.

POST DEFENSE

Several techniques may be taught to players learning to guard an offensive post player in or around the free throw lane. This situation may require either the ball-defender-player closed stance (hand across the passing lane in a ball-you-offensive player) (figure 7.11a) or fronting stance (figure 7.11b). As a general rule, the ball should be kept out of the power zone (post area) using one of these two stances. Note that in a closed stance the hand is in the passing lane (ball-you-player guarded) with thumb down and palm facing the ball.

a   **b**

Figure 7.11 a–b   Post defense. *(a)* Closed stance–high side; *(b)* Fronting stance.

The most common post defense technique is the closed stance, avoiding contact, keeping a hand in the passing lane, and defending in a position on the side of the defender. This "half-front" position is a compromise between keeping the ball out of the post area and being ready to check or block out the post player when a perimeter shot is taken. One added position rule is needed when the offensive post is in the low/medium post position. When that happens, take a position above the post player when ball is above the free-throw line extended and take a closed stance position below or on the baseline side when the ball is below the free-throw line extended (figure 7.12). When the ball changes positions relative to the free-throw line, the defender can choose to go behind the post (easier) or in front of the post (more difficult) to maintain the ball-you-player guarded closed stance position.

When in a fronting stance, the defender should see the ball and stay in defensive stance without contact. This allows the defender to anticipate and move for the pass to the post.

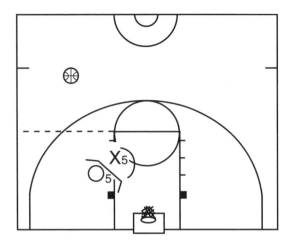 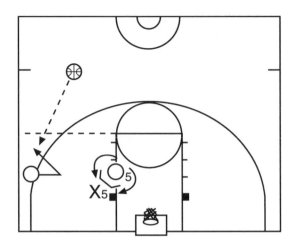

Figure 7.12 Defending the post—closed stance.

Critical Cue

Fronting post—stay in
stance with hands up,
be ready to move
for the pass.

The fronting stance has the advantage of keeping the ball from post players better, but also has the disadvantage of giving the offensive post player a definite edge for rebounding when a perimeter shot is taken.

Offensive post players control defenders by establishing and maintaining contact. Post defenders should avoid contact unless they have an advantage in position; in other words, they should maintain a safe distance from the ballhandler and keep moving. This keeps the offensive post player (and passer) guessing.

The basic fundamentals also apply to defending a post player with the ball; defenders should stay in a defensive quick stance with both hands ready. When an offensive post player does receive the ball in the low or medium post area, the defender should be taught to take a step back and reestablish a ball-you-basket position. Maintaining distance will give the defender reaction time to defend against an offensive post move, also prevent the offensive post player from using contact to control the defender, and allow a teammate time to help from the perimeter.

ON-BALL TO OFF-BALL DEFENSE

Critical Cue

Defender—ball moves,
you move to ball.

When guarding the ballhandler as a pass is made, immediate transition must be made from on-the-ball status (ball-you-basket position) to off-the-ball status (ball-you-player guarded position). This is done by jumping (or exploding) to the ball (primarily) and to the basket (secondarily) to assume a closed or open stance. This is shown in figure 7.13.

OFF-BALL TO ON-BALL DEFENSE

The other defensive transition situation when the opponents have the ball is when you change status from off-the-ball (open stance) to on-the-ball coverage. This technique is called "closing out" to the ball; this occurs when you are in a help defensive position (protecting the basket and supporting the defender on the ball). Then the ball is passed to the player you are guarding. The correct technique for this is described below and shown in figure 7.14:

- Sprint halfway to the player with the ball you are guarding (close out short).
- Break down into a regular defensive stance using active feet (stutter steps) with both hands above your shoulders and above head level. Approach ballhandler with caution, but be aggressive.
- Recommended foot position is with inside foot up (belly to sideline or baseline).
- Close out in a ball-you-basket path (prevent the drive).
- Close out short (keep a gap) with weight back. Throw hands up and back.

The objective on a "closeout" is to prevent penetration (dribble or quick air pass past your head) and then pressure the ballhandler, especially on the shot.

Critical Cue

Close out short to prevent the drive.

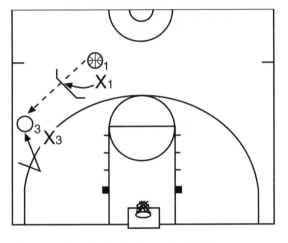
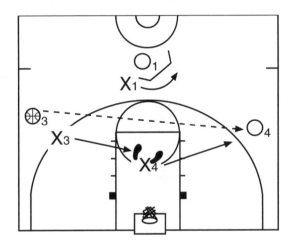

Figure 7.13 Explode (jump) to ball on every pass/dribble move.

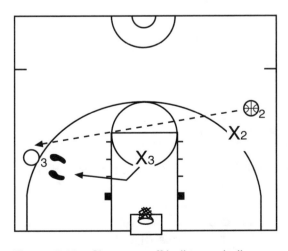
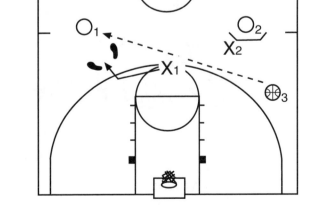

Figure 7.14 Closeout—off ball to on ball.

Coaching Points for Defense

General

- Get in a stance and stay in a stance.
- Use mind, body, feet, and eyes as first tools of defense.
- Prevent easy scores, no lay-ups.
- Keep pressure on the ball, every shot.
- Prevent penetration by the pass or dribble.
- Move on every pass or dribble.
- Take away an opponent's strength.

On the Ball

- Get low and stay low.
- Maintain ball-you-basket position.
- Guard players in a live ball situation: front foot to front foot, hands and feet active, and within touching distance (lead hand up).
- Guard the dribbler, keep head in front, jab with the lead hand, and run to recover when necessary. Force to weak hand.
- Guard a dead ball situation: swarm the ballhandler without fouling or sag away from the ballhandler.
- Jump/explode to the ball when a pass is made.

Off the Ball

- Close out to the ball when it is passed to an assigned offensive player; sprint, break down, and prevent the drive (always close out "short"— prevent the drive).
- Maintain ball-defender-basket position.
- Get in an open (pistols) stance (far from ball) or a closed (hand across/ thumbs down) stance (close to the ball).
- Keep space between yourself and the dribbler, i.e., keep a gap.
- Keep the ball from offensive post players.
- Be able to help and make the decision to bluff or switch on screens, penetrations, or closeouts.

SPECIAL DEFENSIVE SITUATIONS

In addition to the basic skills of defending on and off the ball, there are several other tactics that can help your team defend against special offensive threats.

A situation that occurs mostly on defense but can occur on offense is a loose ball from a bad pass, errant dribble, or any loss of ball control by an offensive player.

The best rule to use for this situation is to get both hands on the ball; if it is in the air use a two-hand pickup and snap the ball to a quick stop-chinit position. If the ball is on the floor, dive on the loose ball with both hands. Remember, playing rules require you to pass to an open teammate before getting up from the floor.

Defenders should use the help-and-decide defensive technique to combat the offensive tactic, which clears out one side of the court for the ballhandler to dribble drive to beat the defender. The off-the-ball defender should be ready to help and decide to help or switch if the defender on the ball is beaten or when his or her assigned player vacates the area.

Critical Cue

Chin a loose ball.

Help and Decide

On clearouts or any penetration situation, the off-ball defenders must make a critical decision: help (protect the basket and cover the penetrating dribble) and decide (to switch defensive assignments, trap with the defender on the ball, or bluff to buy recovery time for the teammate guarding the dribbler). Communication is the key—be ready to help and communicate when you decide. Two options are shown in figure 7.15.

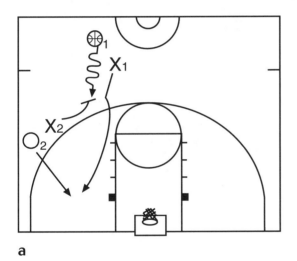
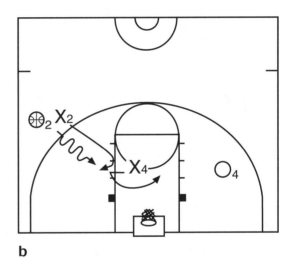

a   b

Figure 7.15a–b Help and decide—on offensive penetration. *(a)* Help and switch, *(b)* help and recover.

Screens

When an offensive player screens or shields a defender to assist a teammate in getting an open shot, special tactics must be used. These include avoiding screens whenever possible—defenders should be in motion when offensive players approach them to set a screen. Screens generally can be defeated by fighting through the screen, in which case a teammate may help out the screened defender with a "show-and-go" move (figure 7.16), or switching assigned opponents, especially when a defender is unable to get through the screen (figure 7.17) or by trapping the dribbler on a screen. Notice that the defender guarding the screener switches "up," calls the switch, and contains the ballhandler.

Figure 7.16a–d Fighting through screens. *(a)* Go over the top, *(b)* helper "shows" to help, *(c)* fight over the screen, *(d)* teammate recovers when offensive player leaves.

Figure 7.17a–b Switch the screen. *(a)* Helper (on right) steps up to switch on player #4, *(b)* helper calls the switch and teammate exchanges assigned players.

Traps

Coaches also may want to develop defensive techniques that can be used to handle an exceptional offensive player or function as a surprise tactic. Trapping occurs when two defenders double-team an offensive ballhandler (two-on-one). Emphasize that both players must stop the ballhandler from escaping the trap by being in good defensive basic position, keeping feet active, positioning themselves knee-to-knee, and keeping inside hands up to prevent a quick air pass. The objective is to force a lob or bounce pass, and players should learn not to reach for the ball or commit a foul. All other teammates off the ball should close off the nearest passing lanes to prevent any passes from the trap into their zones. The best places to set traps are in the corners of the court (figure 7.18).

Critical Cue

Defensive traps—feet active, inside hand up, contain without fouling.

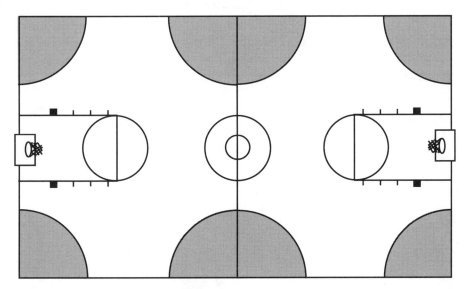

Figure 7.18 Optimal trapping locations.

Defensive Charge

The defensive charge—one of the fundamental defensive plays in basketball—is used when a defender has beaten an offensive cutter to a desired position on the floor and is in a legal guarding position. This defensive skill must be taught properly not only for its great potential as a team play (it can prevent an opponent's three-point play and result in two free throws for the defender), but also because it involves a contact skill that must be developed progressively to avoid injury. The rules that apply to this situation are: the defender is entitled to any spot on the floor that is taken in a legal guarding position; the dribbler needs no room but the defender must be in a legal position before the offensive player's head and shoulders pass the defender's body; away from the ball the offensive cutter must be given the chance to change direction (never more than two steps); the defender always must be in a legal guarding position before a player leaves his or her feet to become airborne; and the defender can move the feet backward slightly and can always protect the body.

Players should be taught these techniques for taking the charge:

1. Get in and stay in a good defensive basic stance and keep feet active.
2. Take the blow in the chest area.
3. Resist giving up an established position, but have most of the weight on the heels.
4. Keep the arms out of the action and use them for protection. This is identical to screen setting technique—protect vital areas.
5. Fall properly—with arms up and in front, the buttocks should hit the floor first, followed by the lower and upper back. Keep the head in a curled position (see figure 7.19).
6. Assume the officials will not call an offensive foul and scramble up to regain basic position.
7. Know when to "take the charge." Disrupt the offensive player's movement, but pick a situation where the offensive player has poor body control and is not alert.

![Basketball ball icon]

Critical Cue

Must be knocked down on the defensive charge.

a

b

c

d

Figure 7.19a–d Defensive charge–falling properly. *(a)* The defender must be knocked down, *(b)* landing–rear end first, *(c)* back roll, head curl, *(d)* scramble to regain basic position.

PRESSURING THE SHOT

A special skill needed when defending the player with the ball occurs when a set/jump shot is taken. Remember, the general rule is to pressure every shot. The technique to do this is as follows:

- Stay in your stance—don't leave your feet until the shooter does.
- Use lead hand to force the shooter to alter the shot—don't try to block it, just make the shooter change the shot.
- Lead hand up in a vertical position with *wrist back* (don't slap down and cause a foul).
- Apply verbal pressure also (shout, make noise, scream, call name). Yell "Shot."

Critical Cue

Pressure every shot—stay down, hand up, wrist back.

DEFENSE DRILLS

Insist on execution first, but demand intensity on defense. Players must learn to play hard individually in order to develop a cohesive team defense.

Moving Stance and Steps

PURPOSE

To develop individual defensive stance and steps.

EQUIPMENT

One ball for coach, half court (minimum).

PROCEDURE

All players are spaced about the court, facing the coach with a clear view. They assume a basic defensive stance at the coach's "palm down" signal and respond to coach's signals and commands with continuous defensive stance and step moves. The coach uses the ball for most signals. The direction moves used are shown in figure 7.20.

Signals/meaning	Movement
Palm down/live ball	Basic stance; active feet
Ball in stomach/back dribble	Slide forward
Ball in right front/dribble drive right	Angle slide right
Ball in left front/dribble drive left	Angle slide left
Finger point left-right/side dribble	Side slide
Ball in triple-threat position, then toss ball on the floor/looseball	Closeout and dive on the floor for loose ball
Ball overhead/dead ball	Stay in stance/hands around ball
Shoot the ball in place/shot	Defenders call "shot" block out and rebound imaginary ball.

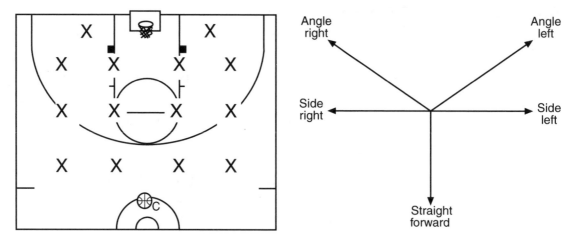

Figure 7.20 Moving stance and steps–direction of movement.

Line Drill: Individual Defense

PURPOSE

To develop individual defensive skills in a progressive manner.

EQUIPMENT

Ball for every two players (at least four balls).

PROCEDURE

Players form four lines on the baseline. Offensive/defensive zigzag (zigzag in pairs). The first player in each line assumes a defensive stance with the next player in an offensive stance. The offensive player zigzags down the floor while the defender maintains defensive distance and a ball-defender-basket position. Players switch positions on the return trip.

OPTIONS

These should be done in this sequence as a learning progression.

- Offensive zigzag—90° change of direction without ball/then with ball (dribbling).
- Defensive zigzag (slides)/using 45° backward defensive slides (lead hand palm up flicking at imaginary ball, trail hand near shoulder/side). On

change of direction, lead with elbow as you rear turn and continue slides at 90° change of direction—go baseline to baseline using swing steps.

- Defensive zigzag—90° change of direction with running steps (simulates getting beaten by the dribbler). The move always starts and ends with sliding steps; slide diagonally left (dribbler gets past), sprint to reestablish position, break down and slide; change direction and repeat (slide-run-slide). Continue baseline to baseline.
- Offensive-defensive zigzag—offensive and defensive pairs. The offensive dribbler first coaches the defender while zigzag moving and carrying the ball to simulate the dribble. Then the offensive player dribbles down the floor (using pullback crossover, regular dribble crossover, spin dribble, or behind the back dribble moves)—make the defender perfect.
- Offensive-defensive zigzag in pairs—live offense and defense in two alleys down the court.
- One-on-one full court—live offense and defense to score; defender slides, runs when needed, turn the dribbler in the backcourt, push to weak hand in frontcourt, maintain ball-you-basket relationship, prevent lay-ups.

On-Ball, Off-Ball Drill

PURPOSE

Teach defenders to adjust quickly to on-ball and off-ball positions while defending penetration (help and decide situations).

EQUIPMENT

Two lines of players, one ball and a half court.

PROCEDURE

Coach starts with ball in middle (both defenders in closed stance), then dribbles to one side as defenders adjust to closed and open stance positions. Coach may pass and offensive players go live or penetrate at any time (figure 7.21). The drill rotation is from offense to defense to back of opposite line.

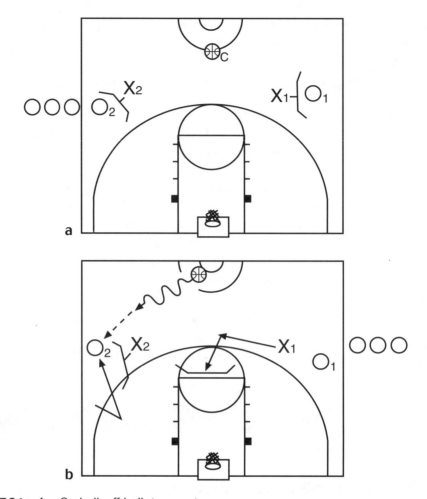

Figure 7.21a–b On-ball, off-ball—two-on-two.

Closeout Drill

PURPOSE

To develop the individual defensive skill of closing out on an off-the-ball offensive player who has just received a pass.

EQUIPMENT

One ball and basket per group; ideally one ball and basket for every two players.

PROCEDURE

When practicing the closeout technique, the defensive player starts under the basket with a ball (figure 7.22). The offensive player is in basic position facing the basket within a range of 15 to 18 feet. The defender passes the ball to the offensive player with a crisp air pass and closes out to defend. The rule is to first prevent the drive by breaking down in the stance halfway to the ballhandler (feet active, inside foot forward, both hands up—palms facing ball). Then pressure the ball and shot, and block out when a shot is taken. From that point, there is a live competition between offense and defense that ends when a basket is made or the defense gains possession of the ball. The dribbler is limited to two dribbles.

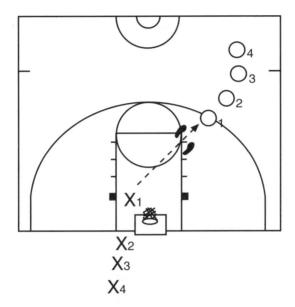

Figure 7.22 Closeout.

OPTIONS

- Closeout—shot only
- Closeout—shot fake, drive only
- Closeout—live offense (rotate lines each time)
- Closeout—live offense and defense (rotate)
- Closeout—live, make it-take it (defense must stop offense to rotate)

Closeout Drills—One-on-One, Two-on-Two, Three-on-Three, Four-on-Four

PURPOSE

To practice all outside moves by perimeter players.

EQUIPMENT

One ball and one basket per group.

PROCEDURE

Form line of players under each basket off the court. The first player steps under the basket with the ball and will be the defender. A line of offensive players is placed 15 to 18 feet away facing the basket. The defender makes a crisp air pass (with feet on the floor) to the first player in the offensive line and then closes out to defend that player. The drill begins as soon as the pass is made for both offense and defense. The perimeter offensive player should catch the ball with feet in the air facing the basket, read and react to the defender's actions and apply fundamentals to shoot or make an outside move.

Players may rotate to the back of the opposite line each time, play make it-take it, or any arrangement of their choice. The drill may be run as a three-on-three option (figure 7.23) that then becomes a teamwork competition with on-the-ball and off-the-ball play. Note the passer guards the ballhandler on the first pass.

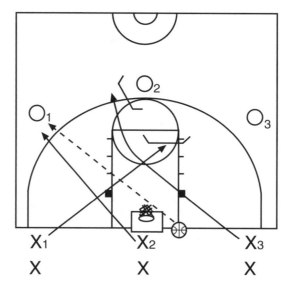

Figure 7.23 Three-on-three closeout—coach passes, closeout defenders cannot cover player in their line, must communicate.

Defensive Slide Drill—Moving Stance/Steps

PURPOSE

To develop individual defensive steps.

EQUIPMENT

Full-court boundary lines.

PROCEDURE

All players begin drill in court corner and use defensive steps as described. They follow the path noted in figure 7.24. Players should allow the preceding player to reach the adjacent free throw line before starting. The drill should include the following 10 movements:

- Forward slide
- Slide left
- Close out to baseline
- Slide right
- Angle slide-run-slide

- Slide right
- Close out to the half-court line
- Face belly to the sideline with an angle left side
- Face belly to the sideline/baseline with an angle right side
- Close out to the free throw line

Players repeat the circuit starting from the left side of court. They complete one circuit starting at each corner of one end line. It may be desirable to record the time it takes to complete the circuit after using the drill several times.

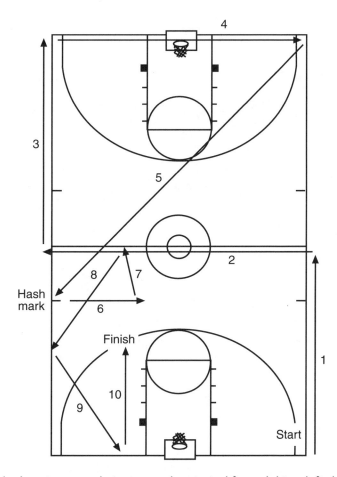

Figure 7.24   Moving stance and steps, may be started from right or left side.

Two-on-Two, Three-on-Three, Four-on-Four Half-Court Drills

PURPOSE

To develop individual defensive skills in a team setting.

EQUIPMENT

One ball, half court.

PROCEDURE

Three (or four) offensive and three (or four) defensive players playing a half-court game centered around different offensive moves and situations to be played by the defender. Start with different sets and situations.

OPTIONS

- Screens (on-ball/off-ball)
- Post play
- Penetration
- Closeouts
- Traps
- Charges

Four-on-Four Half Court Plus Transition

PURPOSE

To develop individual defensive skills in a team setting and make transition from defense to offense after defensive rebounding.

EQUIPMENT

One ball, full court.

PROCEDURE

Begin play as four-on-four half court, defending against any offensive situation desired. When defenders successfully gain the ball on a steal or a defensive rebound, they may fast-break to score at the other end of the court. Four new defenders then take positions, and the successful defenders now come to the original half court as offensive players.

8

Rebounding

"Offense sells tickets, defense wins games, rebounding wins championships."

—Pat Summitt, University of Tennessee Lady Volunteers (six-time National Champions)

In basketball, rebounding may be defined simply as gaining possession of the ball after a missed-shot attempt. It is important for players to learn both offensive and defensive rebounding skills: The objective of offensive rebounding is to maintain possession of the ball while defensive rebounders attempt to gain possession of the ball after the offensive team has attempted a shot. Rebounding is a major part of the game at all levels. In fact, it may even have a greater influence on a game played by younger players because of the higher percentage of missed shots at the beginning level.

REBOUNDING TOOLS

Rebounding, like playing defense and moving without the ball on offense, requires determination and discipline. Although height and jumping ability are advantages, the keys to rebounding are determination and technique. Statistics on the leading rebounders in professional and college basketball are not merely a list of the tallest players or the ones with the highest vertical jump. It has often been stated that most rebounding, even in college and professional basketball, is done "below the rim". Positioning and being quick to the ball (horizontal movement), not leaping ability (vertical jumping), may be the most essential skill for rebounding. The same is true at the high school and grade school levels. Rebounding requires more than physical tools; considerable effort and proper execution of skills are necessary.

Joan Crawford was a 5-foot, 11-inch center who was an AAU star in the 1950s and 1960s as she led her team and competition in rebounding. She led her USA team to the 1957 World Championship and was inducted into the Naismith Hall of Fame in 1997. Denise Curry at 6 feet, 1 inch, also a 1997 Hall of Fame inductee, holds the UCLA rebounding record and was the 1981 USA Player of the Year, a Gold Medal Olympian, and was named "French Player of the Decade" for the 1980s. Dennis Rodman came from a small NAIA school in Oklahoma and has led the NBA in rebounding many years. He is only 6 feet, 8 inches, small for an NBA frontcourt rebounder.

Without question, certain physical attributes are advantageous to rebounders. Players who are tall, have long arms, large hips, and well-developed leg and upper-body musculature are going to have an advantage over other players.

Vertical jumping ability is undoubtedly an asset for a rebounder. Coaches must see to it that all players learn rebounding skills, not just jumping skills. This does not mean that you should not encourage players to develop their jumping ability to its full potential. Use strength programs and other devices to enhance players' vertical jumps in your practices. But in addition to helping them jump their highest, you also must make sure they are jumping correctly. Proper jumping technique involves bending the knees, jumping from both feet, and using the thrust of the arms to reach full extension. Teaching players to jump in this manner will not only develop their leaping abilities to the maximum but will also help them maintain their balance in jumping situations and will reduce the number of over-the-back fouls charged to them when rebounding.

MOTIVATING PLAYERS TO REBOUND

The first step in teaching rebounding is to convince players that it is a skill that is relevant and important for them to learn and perform in game situations. Explain that the entire team—not just those who are tallest, play post positions, or have exceptional jumping ability—must master rebounding skills. Every player can become a good rebounder. If you bypass this initial step, you will probably be disappointed by the rebounding performance of certain players during the season.

Reasons for Rebounding

Give players solid reasons why rebounding is a very important skill for all of them to develop. They must come to see rebounding in terms of its importance in getting and maintaining control of the ball and its key role in team offensive production. Rebounding is also a critical part of team defense, the final phase.

Ball Possession.   Rare is the player who does not like to shoot the basketball. Although it may sound simplistic, remind players that they can't shoot if they don't have the ball. Rebounding is the primary way of gaining or maintaining possession of the ball.

At the offensive end of the court, offensive rebounds to maintain possession frequently lead to quick and easy baskets.

Fast Break.   The ability of a team to begin a fast break depends entirely on defensive rebounding and turnovers by opponents. That is why teams with a well-developed fast break are also teams that have effective defensive rebounders. Whether your team offensive style is fast or slow, your basic strategy should emphasize getting the ball up the court quickly. This prevents opponents from sending their whole team to the basket for an offensive rebound on a shot attempt.

Players usually like to fast-break, so it should be easy to motivate them to concentrate on rebounding. Put it to them in simple terms: No rebounds, no fast break. Rebounds = fast breaks.

The fast-breaking Boston Celtics of the 1960s were at their best when triggered by Bill Russell, one of the best college and professional rebounders in history.

Winning.   Perhaps the strongest evidence of the importance of rebounding you can present to your players is the high correlation of successful rebounding with winning basketball games. One study examining rebounding and winning over a 10-year period found that teams that out-rebounded their opponents won 80 percent of the time. National leaders in team rebounding win more of their games than do teams that lead the nation in field goal and free throw accuracy. This statistic suggests that teams who gain possession of the ball only after their opponents score will at best trade basket for basket with them. The effective rebound allows a team to pull ahead.

Reinforcing the Motivation

It should be rather easy to convince players why they must rebound if they understand that rebounding is essential for ball possession and the fast break, and that it is very important to winning.

Praise and encourage players who give maximum effort in rebounding, and single out individual players for particular rebounding accomplishments (e.g., most rebounds in a half, most defensive rebounds for the game, best blockout, etc.). Make sure they know how much their coach and teammates value rebounding as a team skill and that their efforts to perform well in rebounding will be rewarded.

After making certain that all players feel responsible for rebounding and that they understand why they must rebound, explain and demonstrate the fundamental rebounding skills.

GENERAL REBOUNDING TECHNIQUE

The suggested rebounding technique requires that players gain inside position on an opponent, block out the opponent, and then get the rebound. Although rebounding seems to consist of three distinct phases, these occur as quickly as if they were a single action. The rebounding technique is commonly referred to as blocking out and is sometimes called "boxing out" or "checking" an opponent.

All players should understand the following fundamental rebounding principles associated with blocking out. They are discussed individually in the sections following the list.

- See the shot.
- Assume the shot will be missed.
- Locate the opponent.
- Go to the opponent and block out.
- Go to the ball.
- Get and keep the ball.
- Move the ball out or down the court.

See the Shot

Critical Cue

Visual contact until physical contact on rebounds.

Players must be aware of when and where a shot is taken. Whether they are guarding an opponent on defense or attempting to get open on offense, they should know where the ball is at all times. Reemphasize to players the need to position themselves so they can see both their assigned player and the ball on defense and use their peripheral vision while moving to get open on offense. Players who are "blind" to the ball usually have other problems with fundamental skills such as positioning and movement that should be corrected.

Once they see a shot is being taken, players should call out "shot" to alert teammates who may have momentarily lost sight of the ball that they should get in position to rebound. Sometimes the shooter will call out "short" or "long" to give a teammate an edge on an opponent for position. The defender guarding the shooter has primary responsibility for making the defensive call. However, none of these verbal alarms are as effective as a player's own observation of the shot being released.

Assume the Shot Will Miss

Remind your players that every shot attempt means a potential rebound. Players must learn to always assume that every shot will be a miss and go to their rebound assignment. The "assume" principle is the most important rebounding guideline.

Find the Opponent

Almost without exception, young players fall into the habit of watching the flight of the ball when shots are in the air. This can prevent them from being able to gain an advantage in rebounding position. Once the ball is in the air, their first reaction should be to locate the opponent they are responsible for blocking out or the opposing player nearest to them.

This does not mean that players should not be aware of the direction and distance of the shot, but they must avoid becoming spectators when the ball is in the air. Train players to be active rebounders by teaching them to locate an opponent while maintaining a sense of the direction and timing of the shot. Move your feet; rebound with your feet.

One way to find out if players are only watching the shot in flight is to use a simple rebounding drill. In this drill, the opposing player holds up a given number of fingers after the shot is released by another player. After rebounding the ball, the player guarding the offensive player should be able to report the number of fingers the opponent held up. If not, the player probably was focusing too much on the ball in the air and not enough on the opponent.

Critical Cue

Assume is the most important rebounding principle.

Go to the Opponent and Block Out

Everything the player has done to this point has set the stage for the next step, the actual blocking out of the opponent. Your players may not have a difficult time with the first three steps, but blocking out an opponent is challenging for almost all players and especially difficult for beginners.

The purpose of blocking out is to gain a positional advantage over an opponent for a rebound. Under normal circumstances, a player is more likely to rebound a missed shot if positioned closer to the basket than the opponent. This is called inside position, because the player is between the basket and the opponent (opponent-you-basket).

Occasionally—when an opponent is far underneath the basket and a shot is taken from a long distance, for example—outside position (opponent between player and the basket) is preferable. Because this rarely happens, for our purposes in this chapter, the inside position is the desired position for a player while blocking out an opponent. Figure 8.1 illustrates the difference between inside and outside positions.

Figure 8.1 Inside and outside positions.

Before actually blocking out, a player must go to where the opponent was previously located, as in figure 8.2. The player should move quickly and not allow the opponent to gain positional advantage. Teach players to use pivots and turns to help them gain inside position for the blockout.

Figure 8.2　Go to the offensive player to block out.

When blocking out an opponent, a player must be in a stance similar to quick stance with the following modifications. Feet should be parallel and shoulder-width apart; arms should be raised, upper arm parallel to the floor, and bent at the elbows; and hands should be palms up/forward. Figure 8.3 shows the standard blockout position.

The blockout is the phase of the rebounding sequence where players usually make contact with an opponent. Contact is normally initiated by the player with inside position. Because players must turn to the basket and be in quick stance to rebound the ball (having already located the designated opponent after the shot was released), they will no longer be able to see the opponent being blocked out. Players must use another sense, the sense of touch, to keep track of the opponent's location. The buttocks, back, upper arms, and elbows are used most often for this purpose.

Figure 8.3　Block out—make contact with hands up.

Figure 8.4 and figure 8.5 illustrate the preferred technique—go to the opponent, use a front turn to step into an opponent's path (right foot to right foot or vice versa) followed by a rear turn to make contact and take away the opponent's momentum. Be proactive—go to the opponent.

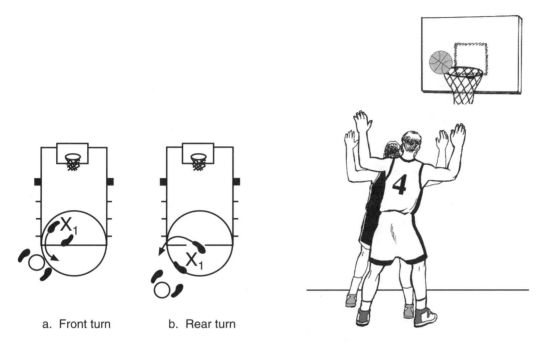

a. Front turn   b. Rear turn

Figure 8.4 Front/rear turn blockout.

Figure 8.5 Rear turn completion of blockout–contact.

Figure 8.6 illustrates why it is so important that players make contact with the opponent. Notice in figure 8.6a that no contact was made, and as a result, the opponent has a clear lane to the basket and an advantage for the rebound. The player in figure 8.6b, however, established contact and prevented the opponent from gaining inside position for the rebound.

Despite widely held perceptions, basketball is a contact sport. Coaches must bear in mind that some players may be better prepared than others for the physical side of rebounding. In drills and games, match up your players according to size, strength, and readiness for contact.

Go to the Ball

The old saying that certain players have a "nose for the ball" may be true. Some rebounders just seem to be in the right place for a rebound on every missed shot. Part of their success may be due to some kind of rebounding instinct. More likely, however, is that these apparently instinctive rebounders have studied where shots taken from various places on the court are likely to go when they are off the mark.

Help your players develop a rebounding instinct by pointing out the rebounding distribution diagrammed in figure 8.7. Note that shots taken from the side of the court are much more likely (70-75 percent of the time) to rebound to the opposite side. Players should learn to take a position on the opposite side of

Critical Cue

Defensive rebounding—go to opponent and make contact with a front turn/rear turn move.

Figure 8.6a–b   *(a)* Contact not made, *(b)* contact made.

the basket from where the shot was taken (known as the weak-side or help-side position). However, they should be taught that shots taken from the middle of the court more often tend to rebound to an area in the middle of the lane. Also, make sure players know that shots taken from close range will rebound closer to the basket than shots launched from long distances. Finally, players should be aware that some rims tend to make the ball rebound farther away from the basket, whereas others seem to cushion the impact of shots and produce much shorter rebounds. Have players test the bounce of the rims during warm-up to find out whether they are likely to produce short or long rebounds.

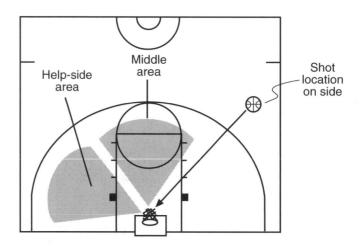

Figure 8.7   Rebound distribution areas.

Finally, three-point field goal shots will rebound a longer distance; shots from in front (top of the key) will rebound near the free throw line and shots from the side generally will rebound outside the free throw lane on the opposite side of the court.

Another explanation for the success of some players to get to the ball is hustle. Players who are good rebounders are not lazy! They take the approach that every free ball is theirs. These players are telling opponents, "I want it more than you do." Inspire this mentality in your players by giving praise and other rewards for coming up with the most rebounds, loose balls, and steals.

Timing and jumping ability are two helpful attributes for rebounding. However, all the spring in the world means nothing if a player does not know when or how to use it. There are several useful drills for helping players get a feel for when they should leave the floor for a rebound. One especially effective drill is to simply have players repeatedly toss the ball off the backboard and attempt to grab the rebound at the maximum height of the jump each time. See "Rebounding Drills" for additional drill ideas.

Get and Keep the Ball

All too often a player will make a perfect rebounding play, only to lose possession because of poor ball protection. When teaching rebounding, emphasize to players that all their efforts to gain possession of the ball are for naught if they fail to protect it afterward.

Figure 8.8 shows how a player should capture the rebound. Using this two-foot jumping, two-hand grabbing, strong, balanced technique for rebounding will reduce the chances of the ball slipping out of the player's hands or of an opponent dislodging it from their grip. Help players develop this skill by insisting that they go after every rebound in this manner. Remind young players to keep their eyes open and focused on the ball as they capture the rebound.

Occasionally the ball may come off the rim in an area where the player is unable to grasp it with both hands. In such cases players should attempt to either gain control using only one hand (block and tuck with two hands) or tap the ball to a teammate.

Maintaining possession of the rebound once it is captured is frequently more difficult than it might seem. Opposing players will try to knock the ball out of the rebounder's hands. Often they will trap the rebounder with two or even three players,

Critical Cue

Rebound from two feet with two hands.

Figure 8.8 Capture the rebound. Always use two hands and two feet when possible.

Critical Cue

The most important technique of rebounding is chinning the ball.

making it nearly impossible for the player to pass or dribble the ball. It is very important that players learn to handle such situations.

When players rebound the ball in the vicinity of an opponent or opponents, their first move should be to bring the ball in under the chin with the elbows out and a hand (with fingers pointing up) on each side of the ball, gripping it tightly (see figure 8.9). This is called "chinning" the ball. Tell your players to "chinit" on rebounds and whenever handling the ball in a congested area. This allows them to capture and retain control of the ball. Tell players not to swing the elbows around to ward off an opponent because this constitutes a violation or foul. They may take up space to clear their area with elbows out (make yourself big). Also tell players to keep the head up and look for teammates breaking downcourt or to an open spot in the backcourt.

Figure 8.9 Chinit—elbows out, fingers up (side view, front view).

Critical Cue

Don't drop the ball to the floor on a rebound—chinit.

The most common situation facing a rebounder who gains possession of the ball after a missed shot is one in which a single opponent (usually one that the rebounder has blocked out) is nearby and attempts to steal the ball or pressure the rebounder. Teach your players to pivot away from the opponent, as shown in figure 8.10. Then the player should either have an open passing lane to a teammate or be able to dribble without having the ball stolen. Caution your players not to put the ball on the floor immediately after rebounding a shot in traffic. This presents a very good opportunity for an opponent to steal or deflect the ball.

When rebounders find themselves surrounded by two or more opponents, the one thing they must remember is not to panic. If they are trained to remain calm, keep the ball in the protected position, and look over the entire court, options will present themselves. One escape move you can teach players is the step-through technique shown in figure 8.11. This technique can be used when the defenders trapping the player leave an opening large enough for the player to slither through. Sometimes an overhead pass fake will cause defend-

front turn

Figure 8.10 Pivot away from pressure.

Figure 8.11 The step-through move.

ers to leave their feet and create an opening that the offensive player can step through or dribble through. Players should not try to force their way through the defensive players because this probably would result in a charging foul.

Another option for a rebounder surrounded by opponents is to throw a pass over them. Even smaller players can use this approach if they make the proper fakes prior to the pass. Simple mathematics says that if the rebounder is being trapped by two or more opponents, then a teammate should be open or able to break open to receive a pass. Another strong possibility in this situation is that one of the defenders will reach in and foul the rebounder. Tell players to keep their composure when they are trapped by opponents after a rebound and wait for one of these options to open up. Fake a pass to make a pass is a rule for these situations that is used by Morgan Wootten of DeMatha High School.

Critical Cue

Defensive rebound—go to opponent, block out, go to ball.

Move the Ball

Once possession is assured, the player with the rebound must choose one of the available options. Whatever action the player takes should begin with the head up and the ball in a protected position.

Because the options facing offensive and defensive rebounders differ, post-rebound actions that players will need to master vary accordingly.

OFFENSIVE REBOUNDING

Offensive rebounding is especially difficult if the defensive players are playing good ball-defender-basket defense because they will have the advantage for getting the inside position. However, offensive players can gain an edge by knowing when and where a shot is going to be taken. Emphasize the need for players to anticipate shots by teammates, as well as to react to their own shot. Otherwise, your players will have great difficulty being successful against good defensive rebounders. Trying to get around a rebounder in proper blocking-out position is not always possible. Remind players not to go over the defensive rebounder's back when attempting to get an offensive rebound because this also results frequently in their being charged with a foul.

The primary position objectives (in order of importance) for an offensive rebounder are: get inside position and block out the defender, get at least even with the defender by going to one side and around to the basket, or make contact with the inside defender and nudge him or her under the basket.

Offensive rebounding is so important because it gives the offensive team another opportunity to score. This new life for the offensive team also serves to discourage the defensive players, who realize they have lost a chance to gain possession of the basketball. There are many options available to the offensive rebounder.

Shooting After Rebounding

When a player makes an offensive rebound, the first option is to shoot the ball. When your players get an offensive rebound, they should first look to shoot, or if this is not possible, then to pass to a teammate (passing outside for a three-point field goal attempt is a good option) before finally exercising the option of dribbling (action over reaction). Emphasize that this is a very good time to take advantage of the defense. Because the defensive opponent was unable to prevent the offensive player from getting in position for the rebound, the defensive player may also be in poor position to defend against a shot. Among the types of shots an offensive rebounder can take are shots without dribbling and shots after dribbling.

Tips.   If your players are well-skilled and big enough, they should tip the ball back at the basket. Tipping is actually a misleading term for a leaping player shooting a rebounded ball before returning to the floor. Tips that involve merely slapping at the ball with one hand are usually unsuccessful. Teach players to catch the ball with elbows locked and shoot it with both hands, if possible.

Tipping the ball is the most efficient way of taking advantage of the defensive players being out of position. By not bringing the ball down from the jump, offensive rebounders take away the defender's chance to recover and give them almost no chance to block the tip attempt. Make sure your players are physically mature and skilled enough before suggesting the tip as a rebounding option.

Shots Without Dribbling.   Encourage players to go up with the shot after a rebound without putting the ball on the floor. Dribbling takes time and allows the defense to recover. It also exposes the ball to the defense, making it more likely that a defender will steal or deflect the ball. If players have learned the correct rebound jumping technique, they should land with the ball ready to go back up for the shot. They can shoot the ball from an overhead position (on the forehead) or chinit position, but should always keep the ball up.

Often players develop the bad habit of dribbling the ball right after they get it, be it from a pass or a rebound. This is a habit that must be broken. Conversely, make a point of noting instances when players do not put the ball on the floor after rebounding, and praise them for this.

A good time to help players develop the habit of going back up with a shot after a rebound is during their individual shooting practices. Tell them that on every missed shot they should hustle for the rebound, get their balance and, with shoulders square to the basket, go back up with another shot (with or without a shot fake). They should continue to shoot and rebound until they make the basket, then start over from a new spot on the court. Shooting without dribbling after an offensive rebound then will become an automatic response.

Shots After Dribbling.   Although it should be avoided whenever possible, there are times when it is acceptable for a player who has grabbed an offensive rebound to dribble before shooting. One obvious example is when a player grabs a rebound far away from the basket and has an open lane to the goal. Because this situation presents an easy scoring opportunity, tell your players to dribble the ball in for the lay-up when the path to the basket is clear. Another option is dribbling out of the lane to clear the ball.

Passing After Rebounding

Another option available to the player who has captured an offensive rebound is to pass the basketball to a teammate. The pass is the second option (after shooting) players should look for after getting an offensive rebound. Thus, when they turn to the basket to look for the open shot after the rebound, they also should locate any open teammates to whom they could pass the ball for an easy shot, especially for a three-point shot. Once again, encourage your players to take advantage of the defensive players' having to recover after the rebound, by either taking a shot or passing to a teammate (usually outside) who has a good shot.

Sometimes an offensive team will choose to reset their offense, either to run a play or to take more time off the clock. In such cases, the option to shoot has the lowest priority for the offensive rebounder, and passing and dribbling become the more preferred options.

Dribbling After Rebounding

In most situations the offensive rebounder should dribble only if a shot or a pass are impossible. Dribbling usually only affords the defensive players an opportunity to recover and possibly steal the ball. Because the offensive rebounder is often surrounded by defenders, the chances of a turnover are even greater. With this in mind, continually advise players to look first for a shot, and then for a passing opportunity before dribbling when they get an offensive rebound.

Critical Cue

Get the offensive rebound, then score, pass, or dribble.

DEFENSIVE REBOUNDING

Good defensive players normally will have a better chance to get inside position because of the ball-defender-basket position they maintain. Because of this positional advantage, and because of the need to limit offensive teams to only one possession each time up the court, there is great pressure on defensive rebounders to claim opponents' missed shots. The defensive rebounder must be adept at blocking out. The most effective way to establish inside position for the defensive rebound is to use front and rear turns. Have players practice these maneuvers alone at first, then against another player acting as an offensive rebounder, and finally against an offensive rebounder with actual shot attempts.

Turns and pivots are not always viable options for defensive rebounders. This is why it is important to emphasize that the key concern in defensive rebounding is not so much what technique is used to block out the opponent, but whether or not the opponent is effectively blocked out. Notice in figure 8.12 how all of the defenders react to the shot by finding an offensive player and then going to the offensive player and blocking out. The defensive players form a weblike screen around the basket that the offensive players cannot penetrate. But if one defensive player fails to block out, there will be a hole in the web and a chance for the offensive team to get the rebound. Blockout position and determination are keys to successful defensive rebounding.

Figure 8.12a–b (a) Before the shot, (b) shot is taken—go, bump, go.

Shooting the ball is not an option for defensive rebounders. However, there are various other options available to defensive players making the transition to offense. The three principal ones are to hold, pass, or dribble the basketball.

Holding the Ball

Having the defensive player simply hold the ball after the rebound may seem pointless. It is not nearly as questionable, however, as having your players rush an ill-advised pass or force their way through opponents using the dribble and risk being called for a charge. Unless your general strategy calls for players to fast-break no matter what, holding the ball tightly under the chin in chinit position after a defensive rebound is sometimes the most prudent move for a player to make.

If players hold the ball in the protective position under the chin following the rebound with knees bent and elbows out, opponents will have to foul them to steal the ball. Defensive rebounders should keep their poise and pivot away from the opponent while maintaining the protective position, and they should always immediately glance down the court to locate an open teammate. Then, if no player is breaking free, they should look for an open teammate in the backcourt in order to pass the ball. Guards must remember to be available and open to receive the ball from a center or forward who is holding it after a rebound. Go get the ball from the rebounder. These rebounders are usually less skilled ballhandlers, and they could easily lose the ball to the opposing team if forced to dribble down the court.

Passing the Ball

The preferred method for moving the ball after a defensive rebound is the outlet pass. No opponent can outrun a sharp pass down the court. Emphasize that this pass is the first option players should look for after a defensive rebound, whether your game strategy calls for a fast break or simply moving the ball quickly.

There are several types of passes used to get the ball to a teammate breaking down the court. The long air pass (also called a baseball or one-handed pass) is used when a teammate is open at the other end of the court. The two-handed overhead pass is used when a teammate is around the midcourt area and there are opponents in the line of the pass. Finally, the two-hand chest pass is used to get the ball to a teammate who has broken open within 10 to 30 feet to the side or to the middle of the court. Because there is often less traffic on the sides of the court than the middle, teach players to look first for open teammates in this area on the rebound side of the court before looking to the middle.

Successful passing is the responsibility of both the passer and the receiver. That is why it is so important that you teach players to get open after a teammate has claimed a defensive rebound. If the opportunity to beat an opponent down the court is available, a player should take advantage of it. Guards should be instructed to move quickly to a spot where the rebounder can get the ball to them. A particularly good spot for guards to position themselves for outlet passes after a rebound is the rebound side of the court between the opponent's free throw line and half-court line (figure 8.13). The outlet guard should have his/her back to the sideline in order to see the whole court.

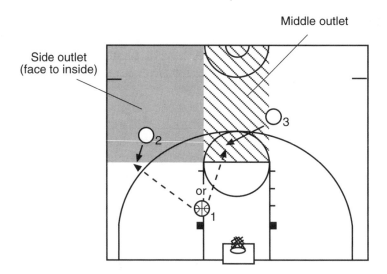

Figure 8.13 Defensive rebound–outlet pass area.

Good basketball teams take care to retain possession of the ball after defensive rebounds. Coaches must emphasize that the transition from defense to offense can lead either to a successful offensive possession or a return to defense, depending on how players handle the ball.

Dribbling the Ball

There are certain players who should not be put in the position of dribbling the ball from one end of the court to the other. In recent years, however, it has become more common for coaches to allow most players on their teams to take a rebounded ball the length of the court using the dribble. As bigger and bigger players develop both the ability to rebound and dribble, the benefits of this full-court maneuver have become apparent.

One major advantage of having a defensive rebounder dribble the ball to the other end of the court is simply that it eliminates the possibility of passing errors. There can be no errant pass if there is no pass. In addition, the rebounder/dribbler can quickly assume the middle position on the fast break without having to wait for a teammate to get open. Players must be able to respond to this situation. Have teammates practice spreading out and filling the passing lanes as they run down the court.

Another big plus in having your defensive rebounders dribble the ball is that it usually creates a numerical advantage over the opposition. Because one or more opponents often are slow to react in making the transition from offense to defense, a defensive rebounder/dribbler can get down the court ahead of them. If players are trained to recognize the situation quickly and hurry down the court, your team frequently can have a five-on-four or even five-on-three advantage.

In general, almost all big players can be taught to rebound, pivot and face up the court, and use one or two dribbles to clear the ball for a pass; and then to use a quick stop and chin the ball when needed.

Coaching Points for Rebounding

- Rebounding is the responsibility of all players on the team.
- Ball possession, the fast break, and winning all are closely associated with good rebounding.
- Assume (a shot will be missed) is the most important principle of rebounding.
- The best rebounding technique emphasizes blocking out the opposing player.
- The blocking-out technique includes the following:
  1. Being aware of when a shot is taken and assuming it will be a miss.
  2. Finding, going to, and blocking out an opponent while paying attention to the direction and distance of the shot.
  3. Going to and capturing the ball and getting it into the protected position under the chin (chin the ball).
- Chinit is the most important technique of rebounding.
- Offensive rebounders should look to shoot, pass, and dribble—in that order.
- Defensive rebounders should either pass, dribble, or hold the ball, depending on their skills and the situation.

REBOUNDING STATISTICS

Keep rebounding statistics for each player and for the team as a whole. Offensive and defensive rebounds should be recorded separately to help identify players having trouble rebounding at a particular end of the court. This information may make you aware of a problem with a player's offensive or defensive rebounding technique, or it might tell you that a player is not hustling enough at one end of the court. Individual rebounding statistics are one of the many pieces of information you should use in evaluating the contribution of each player, particularly those positioned nearest the basket.

An excellent team goal is 60 percent of all rebounds, 30 percent of offensive rebounding situations, and 80 percent of defensive rebounding situations. Percentage goals are better than rebound numbers, because they are valid for all types of play (slow or fast).

REBOUNDING DRILLS

An important part of rebounding is aggressiveness and making legal contact with opponents. Players should be given drills that progressively develop the trait of aggressiveness over time.

Rebound Number

PURPOSE

To practice seeing the opponent and the ball when a shot is taken.

EQUIPMENT

Ball and basket.

PROCEDURE

Divide players into pairs, with two or three pairs per basket. Put two players on offense and two on defense; one offensive-defensive pair on each side of the lane, halfway between the baseline and free throw line. Have a coach at each of the free throw lines with a ball. Defensive player on each side of the lane in basic position guards the offensive player. Offensive players begin to move to get open. The coach can pass to them if they get free under the basket. Otherwise, the coach takes a shot and each offensive player immediately raises a hand and holds up a certain number of fingers as they rebound. The defensive players try to block out the offensive players and get the rebound. If one of the defensive players gets the rebound and both defenders correctly name the number of fingers their offensive opponent held up, the offensive players move to play defense the next time.

Line Drill: Defensive Rebound Addition

PURPOSE

To teach players the techniques of defensive rebounding through simulation.

EQUIPMENT

Half court (minimum).

PROCEDURE

The drill is organized in four lines on the baseline. The coach gives the verbal command "Defensive Boards." The first player in each line sprints on the court 6 to 15 feet from the basket in defensive basic position. The coach designates ball location (left or right). On the command "Rebound," each player simulates the blockout, captures the rebound, chins the ball, and makes an outlet pass. Then the next four players sprint onto the floor in basic position.

VARIATION

Boards in Pairs—the first four players sprint onto the floor in an offensive basic stance in triple-threat position (left or right) near the power zone, and the next four assume a proper defensive basic position to pressure the ballhandler and support the defender playing on the ball. On the command "Shot," all four defenders carry out defensive rebound assignments, and all must make contact. No ball is needed for this drill.

Rebound and Outlet Drill

PURPOSE

To teach players the skill of taking a defensive rebound off the backboard and making an outlet pass (or dribble).

EQUIPMENT

One ball per basket (the drill can be run simultaneously with two lines, one on each side of the basket).

PROCEDURE

This is a defensive rebounding and passing drill. Have the receiver call the passer's name as he or she breaks to get open.

The first player X_1 passes to X_4, gets open for a return pass received with a quick stop in the free throw lane, and tosses the ball underhand above the rectangle level to simulate a defensive rebound (figure 8.14).

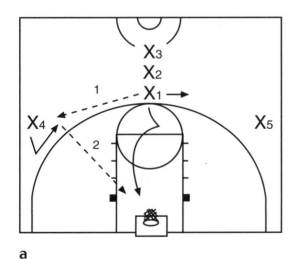
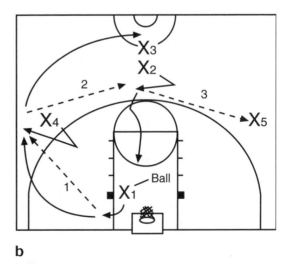

a   b

Figure 8.14a–b Rebound and outlet drill for defensive rebounding: *(a)* start, and *(b)* continuation.

X_1 angle jumps to the ball, captures the ball with two hands, brings the ball to the forehead, makes a front turn on the right pivot foot, makes an outlet pass to X_4, and takes the place of X_4. Player X_4 passes to X_2 and then goes to the back of the line.

The sequence is repeated on the other side with players X_2, X_5, and X_3.

Three-on-Three Closeout and Blockout Drill

PURPOSE

To simulate team competition in a controlled three-on-three rebounding situation.

EQUIPMENT

Ball, basket, and half court.

PROCEDURE

Three offensive players at 15 to 18 feet from the basket and three defensive players under the basket with a ball start the drill. The drill is played as a competitive "make it-take it" exercise that is restarted only when a basket is made. In defensive rebound situations, the defense must clear the ball above the top of the key area before changing to offense. The coach may require the three defenders to stay on defense whenever an assignment is missed.

Line Drill: Offensive Boards Without the Ball

PURPOSE

To teach players the offensive rebounding skills by simulation.

EQUIPMENT

Half court (minimum).

PROCEDURE

The first four players make a "get-ahead-or-get-even" move from basic position, move to the free throw line area, jump quickly, simulate capturing the ball, land in the chinit position, and use a designated scoring move. They repeat this process at the half-court line, the opposite free throw line, and the opposite baseline. The return is made when all groups of four reach the end line. Offensive spacing (15–18 feet) should be kept with the player immediately ahead.

Advanced Figure Eight Rebounding Drill

PURPOSE

To teach players to control the rebound.

EQUIPMENT

One ball per basket.

PROCEDURE

In groups of three players at a basket, the middle player starts the drill with a pass off the backboard (above the rectangle) to the next player. The object is continuous, controlled two-handed tipping or chinit rebounding by the group for a given number of repetitions with players tipping or rebounding and going behind (figure 8.15).

a   b

Figure 8.15a–b   Figure eight rebounding drill: *(a)* starting position, and *(b)* tip and go behind tip catcher.

Most players need to rebound the ball with a two-foot/two-hand rebound and chinit move and then go back up with an offensive scoring move designated by the coach (overhead, power shot, or shot fake and power shot). Note that rebounders' feet should be kept at right angles to baseline (face the baseline) and shoot the ball above the rectangle so it will rebound from the backboard to the next rebounder.

Garbage Drill

PURPOSE

To teach players to score on the offensive rebound.

EQUIPMENT

Two balls per basket.

PROCEDURE

Two lines of players at the free throw line area face the basket with a ball in each line. The first player passes the ball to the backboard with a two-hand underhand toss and rebounds the ball, then uses a designated scoring move. After scoring (and only after scoring), the player passes the ball to the next player in line and goes to the end of the opposite line. Each player assumes a miss and continues until the basket is made.

The scoring moves should be

- chinit and score,
- chinit, fake (lift the ball head high and keep the legs locked), then score, and
- overhead (keep ball on the forehead—two hands), quick jump to score.

A final phase of the garbage drill can be added to teach aggressiveness and scoring in the lane. The coach has one ball at the free throw line and works with two players at a time, one from each line. The coach will usually shoot the ball and players rebound until one captures the ball. The players should use a two-hand rebound or two-hand pickup and chinit on a loose ball. The player with the ball must score in the lane without dribbling while the other player defends. There are no out-of-bounds areas and the ballhandler may use the coach for a release pass (which will be returned if a quick move to get open is used).

NBA (No Babies Allowed) or Survival Rebounding

PURPOSE

To teach players aggressiveness.

EQUIPMENT

One ball per basket.

PROCEDURE

Groups of four to eight players at each basket with three players in the game at one time. If six to eight are used, extra players should be shooting free throws until they are rotated into the game. The coach or manager is positioned at each basket to shoot the ball (intentional missing) and acts as a passing outlet for the rebounder. See figure 8.16. The rules of competition are as follows:

- Play starts with a missed shot.
- All three players attempt to get the rebound.
- The player who obtains the rebound is on offense, and the other two players become defenders.
- Rebounders use scoring moves; all shots must be taken in the free throw lane without dribbling.
- The rebounder may outlet to the coach and get open for a return pass in the lane.
- There is no out-of-bounds boundary for play.
- Three scored baskets allows a player to rotate out (other players retain their totals).
- Significant fouls are the only fouls called by the coach. A player may lose a score by fouling or by not playing defense.

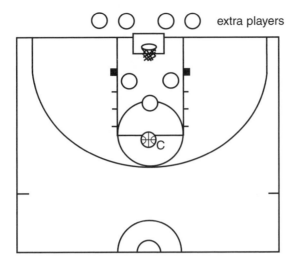

Figure 8.16 No Babies Allowed (NBA) Rebounding.

Individual Rebounding

PURPOSE

Practice rebounding skills by self.

EQUIPMENT

Ball, basket, and tossback rebounding device (or a partner).

PROCEDURE

Carry out rebound options at game speed using two-feet/two-hand rebounding technique.

OPTIONS

- Toss ball against backboard/above rim with a two-hand underhand toss to create a rebound—angle jump to capture ball and make an offensive scoring move (overhead, chin and score, chin—shot fake and score). Assume a miss.
- Toss ball to create a defensive rebound—make a quick outlet pass to tossback or partner.
- Advanced—jump as high as you can and as quick as you can; pop the ball with two hands against the backboard on each jump.
- Place ball on the free-throw lane block—grab with two hands, explode to backboard, and score from two feet. Place on opposite block and repeat.
- Super rebounds—start outside the lane and throw the ball off backboard. Take one step, jump over to get the rebound, and land outside the lane on the other side. Repeat five times and finish with a power move score.

9

Team Offense

Basketball was designed as a game of finesse and reason,
especially on offense. Phil Jackson, longtime coach of
the Chicago Bulls, implored his players to apply this
principle. He used a concept from a Lakota Indian war
chant—"Don't overpower, outsmart."

Coaches should instill in players the confidence to go all out—to have fun, to learn and improve, and to take chances and make mistakes. This is especially true on offense. By preparing players to handle all situations, you will strengthen their confidence that they can be successful.

In order to prepare the team for all situations, the following areas should be covered: general offensive principles, responsibilities of players at each offensive position, offensive team tactics, and special situations for team offense.

GENERAL OFFENSIVE PRINCIPLES

Critical Cue

Team offense must have: high percentage shots, transition, balance, movement, and execution.

Unless you are very familiar with the offensive strengths and weaknesses of team members, you should select a basic offense that can be adapted to a variety of players. It should be flexible enough to allow team members to use their individual strengths. Your basic philosophy should be stable and slowly evolve while your offensive and defensive style of play should change to fit your players.

Any offense should have court balance, that is, it should produce high percentage shots with assigned offensive rebounders and assigned players for defense when a shot is taken. Balance also refers to maintaining proper court spacing—about 15 to 18 feet apart—between offensive teammates. Finally, offensive balance also consists of offensive rebounding and concern for defense when a shot is taken. Making the quick transition from offense to defense (and vice versa) is called developing the transition game. Go to rebound or to defense quickly. Balanced scoring from several players is always better than dependence on a scoring star.

A good offense includes player movement as well as ball movement and may include screening. Scoring should come from the inside (close to the basket) as well as the outside (on the perimeter of the defense). Develop your offense from the inside out; establish an inside game to complement the outside game. This prevents the defense from concentrating on one area or one player. Remember that the execution of any system you design is much more important than the system itself. What your team does is not so critical as how well they do it.

PLAYER POSITIONS AND RESPONSIBILITIES

Each player on a basketball team has a position to play. It is related to role, ability, and skill. The three basic positions in basketball are guard, forward, and center (or post) (figure 9.1). Some coaches use other names such as point, wing, and inside player.

The center is usually the tallest player, with forwards next, and guards being the smallest. Centers and forwards tend to be the best rebounders, while guards are often the best ballhandlers. Guards also tend to play outside more than forwards and centers. No matter what term is used, it is recommended that all perimeter players and all inside players learn the basic skills so they can be interchangeable.

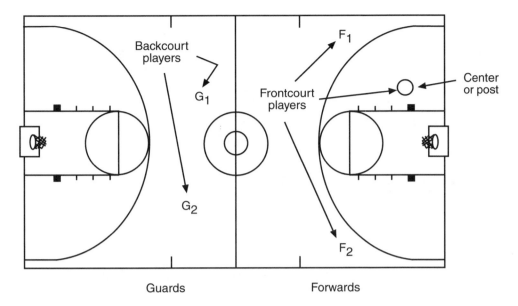

Figure 9.1 Player positions.

Guards

Guards are usually called the team's backcourt when grouped together. This grouping can be broken down further into point guards (normally the best ballhandler and often the player who directs the team on the floor) and shooting guards (also called "big" guards or "off" guards). Because of their dribbling ability, point guards often are able to create a scoring chance for a teammate (such as the shooting guard) by penetrating and passing; that is, by driving past defenders to the basket and passing to an open or unguarded teammate (penetrate and pitch or drive and dish). Point guards are called playmakers because they direct teammates and create scoring opportunities. The point guard usually will be among the best ballhandlers on your team and should also be a leader who can be the coach on the floor. Choose shooting guards from among the best shooters and ballhandlers on your team. Confident shooting or scoring is another important characteristic to look for in a shooting guard.

Forwards

Forwards are sometimes called corner players because their normal offensive position is in the corner of the frontcourt. Most teams play a small forward and a big forward (sometimes called the power forward or strong forward). The small forward is more of a swing player who can play guard or forward and plays facing the basket where good ballhandling is a must. The big forward is often a strong rebounder and swings from outside to inside (back to the basket). Small forwards should be able to play as a combination guard-forward, handle the ball well, play outside on the perimeter, and rebound. Big forwards must be combination forward-centers.

Center or Post Player

Choose players for the center position from among your biggest players who relish playing inside, near the basket, where contact and congestion are readily accepted. The center is usually the biggest player and plays inside around the free throw lane in the high post (near the foul line) or in the low post (close to the basket) and outside the free throw or three-second lane with his or her back to the basket. The center and two forwards are collectively known as the frontcourt.

OFFENSIVE TEAM TACTICS

Develop team tactics to prepare your team to face all basic defensive situations. You will need to include

- a press offense to be used against defensive presses, from half-court to full-court,
- a player-to-player set offense for situations where opponents guard your players individually,
- a zone set offense to be used against zone or area defenses,
- a set offense that can be used against combination defenses (zone and player-to-player),
- a delay or control offense to use when time and score dictate controlling the game and maintaining ball possession for longer periods of time before a shot,
- a transition game—an organized way to go from defense to offense (fast break—this offense keeps the defense honest and puts immediate pressure on the defense) and from offense to defense (prevent opponent's easy scores and fast breaks), and
- special situation plays: jump ball, out-of-bounds, free throws.

Primary Fast Break: Offensive Transition

Critical Cue

Three-lane fast break: ball in middle, side lanes wide, and banana cut to basket.

One way a team can set up a good shot is to run the fast break where the team that gains ball possession brings the ball up the court before opponents can get into good defensive position. The fast break usually develops after a rebound, steal, or possibly after a made basket, and is the fastest way to make the transition from defense to offense. As soon as the defense gains control of the ball, it uses the outlet pass or dribble to start the break—passing being the first option and dribbling the last when moving the ball up the court. Then, the other teammates attempt to beat the defenders up the court while staying spread out. Players should run at top speed under control when fast-breaking up the court. Remember to have one player stay a few steps behind the action in a defensive safety role for balance.

A typical three-lane fast break pattern is shown in figure 9.2. A team needs a three-lane fast break (ball in the middle) when the players outnumber the opponents, three-on-two. When there is a three-on-one situation, the offense should convert to a two-lane fast break (two-on-one plus a trailer), as seen in figure 9.3. In a two-lane fast break, the offensive players should split the floor

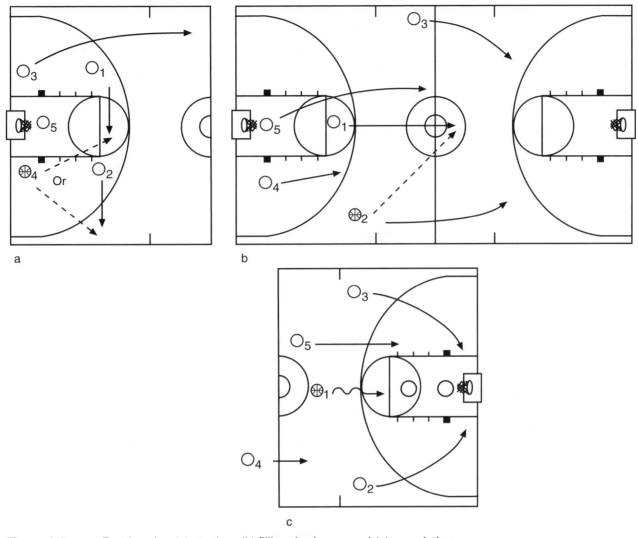

Figure 9.2a–c Fast breaks: *(a)* starting, *(b)* filling the lanes, and *(c)* completion.

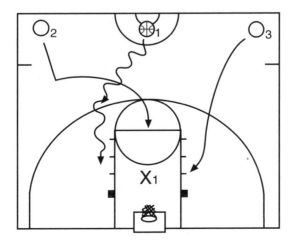

Figure 9.3 Two lane fast break.

(stay at least free-throw lane wide) to make the defender commit. The best ballhandler should handle the ball at the completion—go to glass unless forced to pass. The dribbler always needs to offset the middle to the side of the lane; preferably dribbling with the outside hand. Advanced players can dribble with the inside hand (easier to push bounce pass by defender) and shoot the reverse layback shot if the defender doesn't take the dribbler.

Secondary Fast Break: Offensive Transition

Critical Cue

Two-lane fast break: split the floor and go to the glass.

If a primary fast break (outnumbering the defense three-on-two, three-on-one, or two-on-one) is not available, teams should develop a secondary fast break. This keeps pressure on the defense by taking the ball up the side to the baseline (flattens the defense), posts a player inside, and then reverses the ball to the second side before flowing into the set offense. A secondary fast break is shown in figure 9.4.

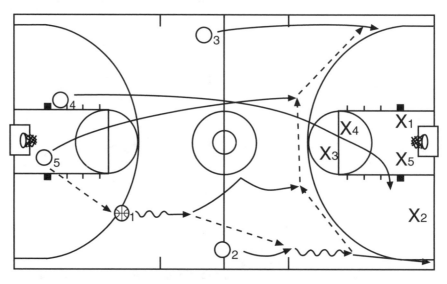

Figure 9.4 Secondary fast break.

Defensive Transition: Offense to Defense

An organized plan is needed to execute offense properly. Then make a transition to defense *quickly* without being outnumbered on the fast break and being able to set your defense.

One method of defensive transition is creating transition roles for all offensive players:

• Fullback—the designated safety, usually the point guard, who is responsible for preventing easy scores (no lay-ups). As any shot by teammates is taken, the fullback sprints to the half-court center circle and retreats, running backward to the basket and directs the defense from there. When the fullback shoots, another player makes the call and switches assignments.

On an offensive fast break, the last player down the floor becomes the fullback and never crosses the half-court line until a score is made or the secondary fast break begins (figure 9.5).

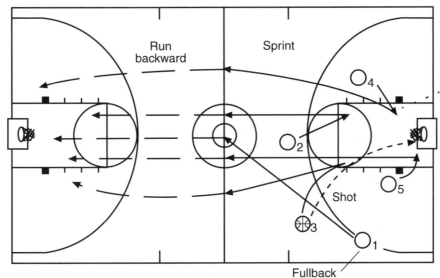

Figure 9.5 Defensive transition.

• Tailbacks—all other players, when the shot is taken, are responsible for going to the offensive boards (assume a miss) until the opponents get the ball or a basket is made. When that happens, all four players sprint to half court seeing the ball over their inside shoulder while running backward to their defensive assignment (if not outnumbered), i.e., they get their "tail" back on defense.

Other variations of the plan can be developed for special situations; i.e., to pressure the rebounder, stop the ball coming up the floor, etc.

Press Offense

Fundamentals such as spacing, cutting, meeting the pass, catching and facing the basket, passing first–dribbling last, etc., are more important than any specific press offense.

If the defense is defending on a full-court (all over the court) basis, you will need a press offense to help your team get the ball inbounds safely. It is preferable to get the ball inbounds before the defense gets set. Designate a frontcourt player to take the ball out after all made baskets and quickly inbound the ball to a guard as shown in figure 9.6. It is preferred that the inbound pass catcher stay out of the corners and not get too close to the sideline (prime trapping areas).

Against any zone press, teach players to attack the defense in the backcourt or frontcourt by having a sideline pass outlet, two middle pass outlets (short and long), and a safety-valve pass outlet slightly behind the ballhandler, as shown in figures 9.6 and 9.7. Emphasize to your players the need to use good passing and catching fundamentals and remind them to move to get open and to keep their poise. Pressing defenses take chances. Players should be prepared to take advantage of those overcommitments.

Generally, players need to attack a pressing defense. Be aggressive and look to score lay-ups by getting the ball up the side or to the middle of the pressing defense.

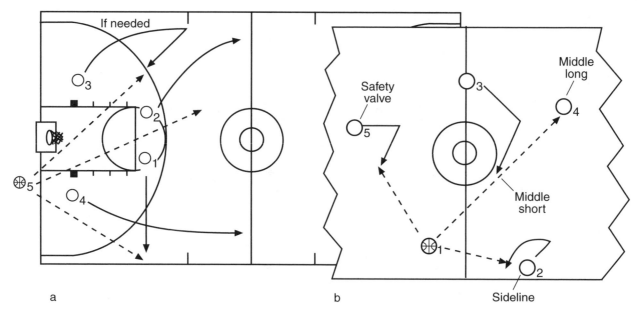

Figure 9.6a–b Press offense—get ball in quickly. (a) Get ball in. (b) Press offense when trapped.

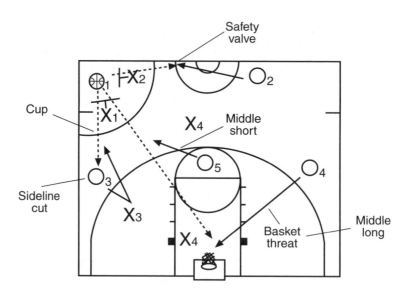

Figure 9.7 Beat the trap: form the three-player cup (O_3, O_5, O_2) with a basket threat.

As a last resort, the offense can use the safety valve to reverse the ball and attack on the second side, as seen in figure 9.8.

In extreme emergencies with the ballhandler in a trap or double team, the nearest teammate (usually the safety valve) can come to the ball directly behind the trap (usually not defended) for a pass. The ballhandler can use a rear turn to protect the ball and make the pass. The "safety valve" player should attack the press immediately.

Set Offense

If the defense is set and waiting after the primary and secondary fast break, a set offense should be used to get a good shot. Your team should get into a basic starting formation and then use the fundamental skill moves with and without the ball to create scoring opportunities.

This basic set or formation may take a variety of starting positions. You should select a preferred starting formation that fits your personnel and favored tactics.

The 1-2-2 "Give-and-Go". One offense for beginning players is the 1-2-2 give-and-go offense. It can be used effectively against player-to-player defenses. The give-and-go offense is a simple team offense that utilizes passing, catching, basic moves without the ball, and individual moves with the ball. The 1-2-2 double low post or open post set is a one-guard, open post formation that allows any player to V-cut into the post area and keeps the middle open for individual offensive moves plus give-and-go options (figure 9.9). The give-and-go offense from the 1-2-2 open post formation can also be used against zone or combination (zone and player-to-player) defenses by depending less on cutting and emphasizing more individual moves from stationary spots.

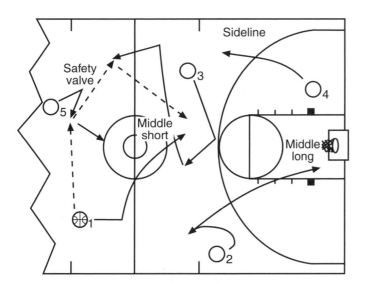

Figure 9.8 Press offense—reverse ball and attack.

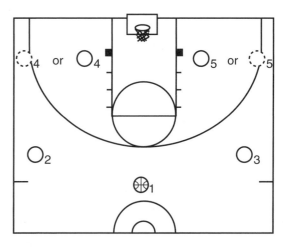

Figure 9.9 A 1-2-2 double low post set (may also be open post).

The rules for this offense are these:

1. The give-and-go from the point to wing pass is a pass and go-to-the-basket move after a V-cut is made by O_3. If the cutting player doesn't receive the return pass, then he or she should "balance the floor" opposite the first pass (figure 9.9a). The give-and-go from the wing position to the corner position is seen in figure 9.9b. Notice how floor balance is regained.

2. If a wing player is overplayed or denied the pass by a defender, your players should use a backdoor cut to the basket and replace on the same side (figure 9.9c). If a corner player is overplayed, he or she should make a backdoor cut and come back to the same side (figure 9.9d).

3. A wing or forward may V-cut into the post area (high or low). When players make ball cuts and don't receive the ball within two seconds, they should return to the same starting position (figure 9.9e).

4. When a shot is taken the point guard (O_1) should go to defense near the half-court line, and the other four players should go to offensive rebounding positions. This rule applies to all offensive situations: The offensive team should always have defensive balance and make a quick transition to defense. Coaches may prefer to have two players change to defense as fullbacks when a shot is taken.

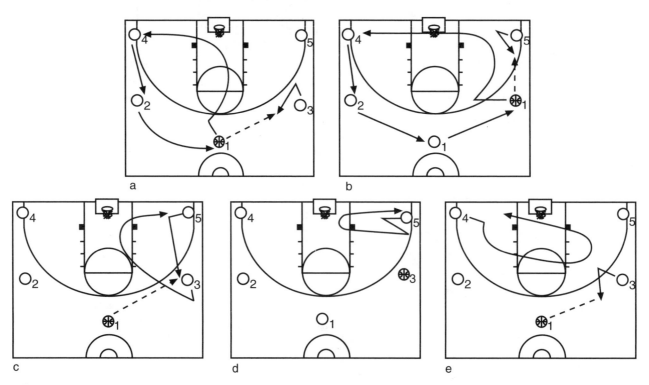

9.9a–e *(a)* Give-and-go from the point. *(b)* Give-and-go on wing-to-corner pass. *(c)* Backdoor cut by the wing. *(d)* Backdoor cut by the forward. *(e)* V-cut to the post area and go back.

The 1-4. The 1-4 double high post set is a formation that requires a good point guard. It is difficult to press, there are four possible entry passes, and the offense needs two inside players (figure 9.10).

The 1-3-1. The 1-3-1 high-low post set has a point guard in front, positions forwards for individual moves, and requires two inside players (the high post must be able to face the basket). See figure 9.11.

The 1-2-2 Stack. Coaches might consider using a 1-2 stack formation. This set calls for a point guard in front, one open side for individual moves, and a stack on the other side. This may be used with one player (O_4) cutting to any position, while the other stack player acts as a screener and then takes up a single post position (O_5). The stack allows a variety of cuts by (O_4), as shown in figure 9.12.

The 2-2-1 or 2-3 Set. The final possibility for an offensive formation is the traditional 2-2-1 or 2-3 set (figure 9.13). This is a two-guard front with a single post (high or low). The side and corner of the court are open for forward moves. The 2-3 formation is more vulnerable to pressing defenses.

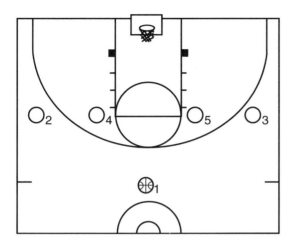

Figure 9.10 A 1-4 set or formation (point O_1, two wings O_2 and O_3, and two posts O_4 and O_5, sometimes called a double high post.

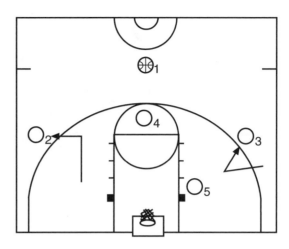

Figure 9.11 A 1-3-1 high-low post set.

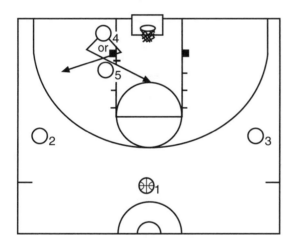

Figure 9.12 A stack set with a one-player front.

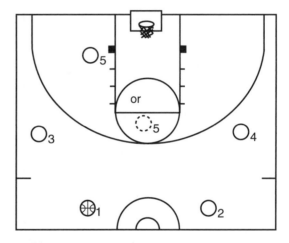

Figure 9.13 A 2-2-1 or 2-3 set (high or low post).

Zone Offense

Against a zone defense, coaches can opt for the modified, recommended give-and-go offense or may select another formation. In any case, teach players to use the following rules:

- Perimeter players align in the gaps on the perimeter and step up into shooting range. (figure 9.14).
- Attack the defense, but be patient. Look for opportunities for dribble or pass penetration inside the zone after passing around the perimeter.
- Watch floor spacing between other offensive players. This spreads the defense and makes it difficult to cover offensive players.
- Cut through zone—one way to test the zone is to move players and relocate as seen in figure 9.15.
- Screen the zone—another effective way to beat a zone defense is to screen inside or outside on the zone, as shown in figure 9.16.

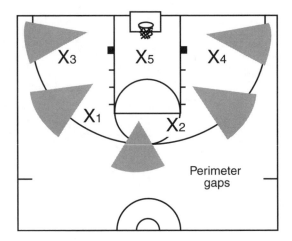

Figure 9.14 Against zone defense, align in the gaps.

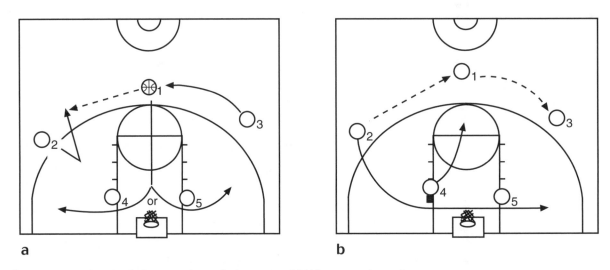

Figure 9.15a–b (a) Point cuts through the zone. (b) Wing cuts through.

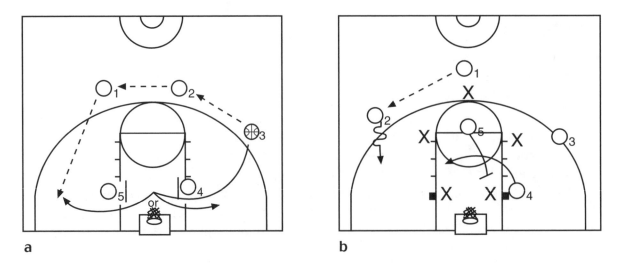

Figure 9.16a–b (a) Screen the zone low. (b) Screen the zone inside.

Coaches also should encourage player and ball movement. Because most zone defenses are ball oriented, ball fakes are also effective. This is a situation where a player should put the ball overhead in order for the defenders to see the ball and react to a fake (pass or shot). Fake a pass to make a pass. The ball is only placed overhead after catching and pitting the ball.

OFFENSE AGAINST COMBINATIONS

When combination player-to-player and zone defenses are used (triangle-and-two, box- or diamond-and-one), you need an organized approach to attack them. The regular player-to-player offense can be used or the zone offense—it is necessary to use an offense that has player movement, ball movement, and screening action. Analyze the defense and use the offense (play or set) that exploits that defense. For example, figure 9.16a could be used with the offensive player guarded one-on-one defensively being the baseline runner using the screens.

Control or Delay Offense

When the team has a lead late in the game, coaches may decide to have players spread out on the court and use the whole frontcourt to make the defense cover a larger area. This is called a delay game (or control game), and usually only close-to-the-basket shots are taken.

In these situations it may be best to run a normal offense with stricter rules on shot selection, or to make a certain number of passes before a shot is taken (unless a lay-up). This offense can be used with or without a shot clock.

When a shot rule is applied until 8 to 10 seconds remain, then the ballhandler looks for dribble penetration and other players start individual moves to set up a good shot. Time and score will dictate when the team should control the ball and use the clock (delay-game tactics). The most common formation for this offense is shown in figure 9.17 where four offensive players are placed in the four corners and the best dribbler is out front in the middle of the court. Player O_1, usually your point guard or playmaker, constantly looks for chances to penetrate and pass. All offensive players should read and react to the defense, and wait for their defender to make an error they can capitalize on. Be sure to have good free throw shooters playing when using your control game, because defenders may foul more, either out of frustration or by design.

Stay on the attack, don't get passive and lose momentum. You can decoy the defense by appearing to delay but always looking for chances to score. If you don't want to shoot, run your normal offense and act like you are attacking.

With 8 to 10 seconds left, a special play may be used (figure 9.18). The options would be O_1 using the pick, O_2 or O_3 moving for the penetrate and pitch three-point field goal attempt, O_4 using the backpick by O_5, and O_5 stepping out after the screen.

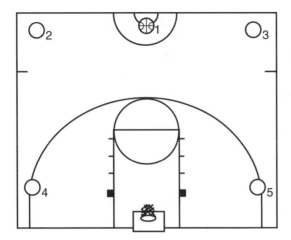

Figure 9.17 Four-corner offense—delay or control game.

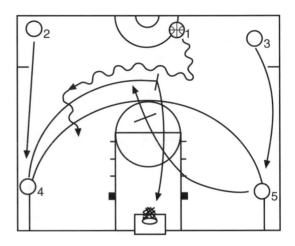

Figure 9.18 Last second score.

SPECIAL SITUATIONS FOR TEAM OFFENSE

Team offense should be prepared to face a variety of special situations: out-of-bounds plays, free throws, jump balls, and last-second scoring plays.

Bringing the Ball Inbounds

Every team must have a plan for bringing the ball into play underneath its own basket and on the sidelines. Examples of formations and plays are shown in figures 9.19 and 9.20, respectively. These can be used against any defense. Most importantly, your team needs to be able to inbound the ball safely against all defensive tactics.

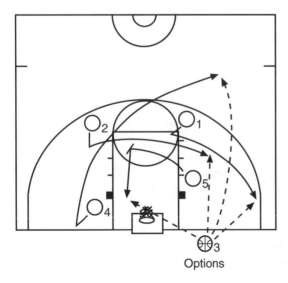

Options

Figure 9.19 Under out-of-bounds play. O_5 and O_2 run and pick-and-roll.

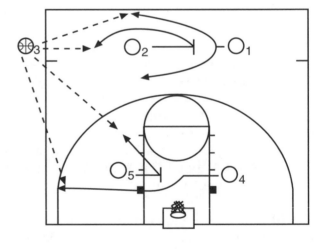

Figure 9.20 Side out-of-bounds play. O_2 screens for O_1, O_5 screens for O_4, and O_3 has four passing options.

Free Throws

Free throw situations also must be planned carefully. On an offensive free throw, the two best rebounders should occupy the second lane spaces and attempt to gain an offensive rebound in the middle of the lane or to the baseline side of the defender. Player O_3 is stationed in a position to be alert for any long rebound or loose ball that might be tipped out, and O_1 and O_3 have safety (fullback) responsibilities on defense and must not let any opponent get behind them for a long pass reception (figure 9.21). For a defensive free throw situation player X_1 is the playmaker who must be alert for a loose ball or long rebound. Player X_2 blocks out or checks the shooter by getting between the shooter and the basket. Players X_4 and X_5 check the opponents on their side of the lane (second lane space) while player X_3 rebounds in the middle area (figure 9.22). When a defensive rebound is captured, all team members make a transition to the fast break.

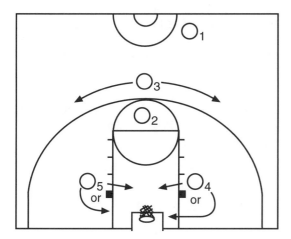

Figure 9.21 Offensive free throw. O_2 is shooting, O_4 and O_5 occupy the second lane spaces on each side, O_3 is at top of circle (key), and O_1 is defensive safety.

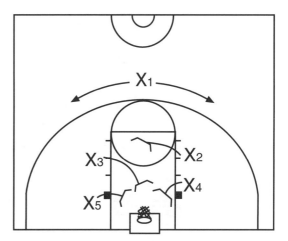

Figure 9.22 Defensive free throw. Four defenders block out or check their opponent on the free throw lane.

Jump Balls

Special plays should be developed for jump ball situations to start games and overtime periods. The smaller, quicker players defend the basket. No matter what the formation, the ball should be tipped to an open spot (where two teammates are next to each other without an opponent in between). See figure 9.23.

Last-Second Shots

The last-second shot situation, diagrammed in figure 9.24, may be used in the delay game or in any situation where a move to the basket is made with 8 to 10 seconds remaining, depending on the level of play (younger players need more time). This allows time for a good shot opportunity, a possible offensive rebound, and a second shot, but not enough time for the opponent to get a good shot at the other end of the court.

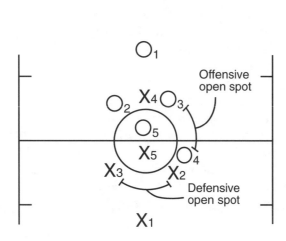

Figure 9.23 Jump ball.

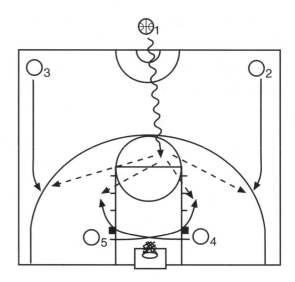

Figure 9.24 Last-second shot. O$_4$ and O$_5$ cross under basket (left hand touching left hand), while O$_2$ and O$_3$ slide into scoring position ready to shoot. O$_1$ has four passing options.

No matter what offensive situation, formation, play, or system is chosen, remember that execution is the key—it is not what players do but how well they do it that is important. Practice these special situations using the clock.

Coaching Points for Team Offense

- Be quick, but don't hurry—focus first on execution and timing, speed later.
- Maintain balance in all areas:
    1. Individual—physical and emotional.
    2. Offensive and defensive.
    3. Offensive rebounding and defensive coverage (on all shot attempts).
    4. Floor spacing—spread out and move the ball.
    5. Inside and outside scoring.
    6. Passing and scoring.
- Teach intelligent teamwork on offense.
- Teach players to put the team first.
- Encourage players to play fearlessly—to make mistakes, but learn from them.
- Individual play should be developed within the team context.
- Ball and players should move on offense. Players should move with a purpose.
- Be patient with team offense. Play must be coordinated with player movements, so learning progress will be slower than with team defense.

Team Offense Checklist

☐ General principles developed
☐ Positions and responsibilities defined
☐ Offensive fundamental skills
☐ Body control
☐ Ballhandling
☐ Shooting
☐ Perimeter play
☐ Post play
☐ Rebounding
☐ Press offense

☐ Primary fast break
☐ Secondary fast break
☐ Player-to-player set offense
☐ Zone set offense
☐ Combination set offense
☐ Delay/control offense
☐ Special situations
    ☐ Jump balls
    ☐ Offensive free throws
    ☐ Out-of-bounds plays

TEAM OFFENSE DRILLS

Team offense should first be executed slowly and correctly. Then, game-speed moves are carried out to develop team coordination and timing.

Skeleton Offense Drill: Five-on-Zero

PURPOSE

To teach basic team offensive formation movements and assignments.

EQUIPMENT

One ball, five players, and half court.

PROCEDURE

Five players at a time take the court to practice team offensive formations, plays or movements, and individual assignments within the team offense. The offense should be initiated from all situations: backcourt, frontcourt, out-of-bounds, and free throws. Offensive play should be completed with a score each time (rebound each shot), and transition should be made to half court.

This is a drill with five offensive players at a time and no defenders.

OPTIONS

- Half-court offense—all sets
- Half court to full court (defense to offense)—after made/missed baskets
  press offense
  secondary fast break
  set offense
- Half-court defense to full-court offensive options to defensive transition

On all offensive shots, assume the miss and make transition (always rebound until the basket is made).

Five-on-Five Team Offense-Defense Drill

PURPOSE

To teach team offense and defense in a progressive manner that culminates in five-on-five competition.

EQUIPMENT

Ball, basket, and half or full court.

PROCEDURE

Five defenders and five offensive players practice team play. They should practice all offensive situations in order to prevent surprises on game day or night. The progression is to have defenders play dummy position defense, then no-hands defense (may grasp jersey in front), before going to gamelike offense and defense with no restrictions.

Play should continue until the offense transitions to the other end of the floor, i.e., go from half court to full court.

OPTIONS

- half court
- half-court make it-take it, full-court transition on misses
- half court to full court (defense to offense transition—press offense, fast break, set offenses)
- full court—stop for corrections, shooting drill breaks (field goal, free throw)

Blitz Fast Break Drill

PURPOSE

To teach the two-lane and three-lane fast break offensive and defensive fundamentals.

EQUIPMENT

One ball, 10 to 16 players divided into two teams, and a full-court space.

PROCEDURE

The two teams are aligned as shown in figure 9.25 with opposing teams at half court. One team is selected to start on defense at one end of the court with the other team on offense at half court.

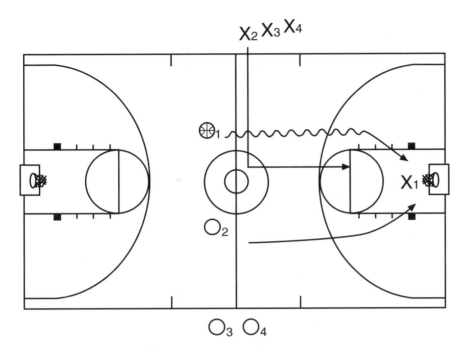

Figure 9.25 Two-on-one blitz fast break.

The drill begins when O_1 crosses half line with the ball for a two-on-one fast break situation with X_2 allowed to help X_1 in the outnumbered situation after touching the center circle. The defender X_1 should bluff, anticipate, and delay the offensive duo in the two-lane fast break until X_2 can recover to help—talk and get both players covered if they don't complete the break.

When the basket is made or missed, X_1 or X_2 captures the ball and advances the ball in a two-lane fast break toward the other basket. As soon as the team of X's gain possession of the ball, the next O player, O_3, touches the center circle and becomes the defensive safety (figure 9.26). When X_2 crosses half line with the ball, O_4 can sprint to defense after touching the center circle. The drill continues to a certain number of baskets, usually 10. Score can be kept on the scoreboard. Coaches should officiate.

The other blitz fast break option is the three lane fast break, three-on-two, where a minimum of 12 players are needed to form the two teams. The alignment is seen in figure 9.27. The two defenders usually align in tandem with the inside player forward (X_4) and the outside player (X_1) covering the basket and taking the first pass on a closeout.

The other defender sprints to help as soon as the middle ballhandler crosses half court. Then dribbler O_1 veer dribbles to one side after "reading" the back defender X_1 and passes to the open teammate. When defenders on the X team get the ball, they form a three-lane fast break to the other end with the ball in the middle. As soon as the X team gains the ball, the next two Os, O_2 and O_5, sprint to defense after touching the center circle. The drill runs continuously until one team reaches 10 baskets.

OPTIONS

- Two-on-one blitz
- Three-on-two blitz

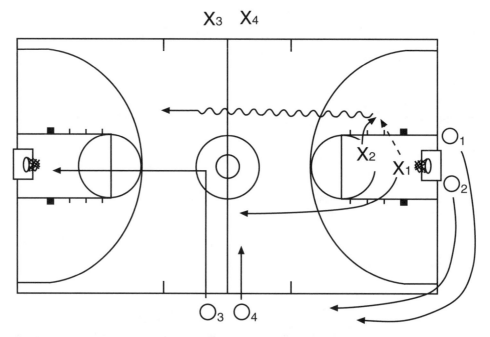

Figure 9.26 Two-on-one blitz fast break.

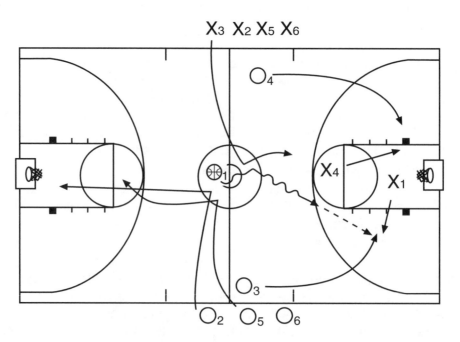

Figure 9.27 Three-on-two blitz fast break.

10

Team Defense

> "Team defense and ballhandling are the cornerstones of successful teams."
>
> — Henry "Hank" Iba, Oklahoma State, Olympic coach, Hall of Fame coach

Critical Cue

Team defense:

- Develop team play.
- Prevent easy scores.
- Be proactive.
- Force alternate offensive options.
- Develop communication.
- Rely on an efficient offense.

Build your team on a solid foundation. Defense is one of the most concrete and unchanging elements of the game. It can be the most consistent phase of team play and should be the heart of your team's strength. A team that prevents its opponents from getting good shots will be tough to beat.

In addition, because younger players have limited individual and team offensive skills, team defense can be an even more dominant aspect for beginners.

Convince players that defense is the key to building a foundation for team play. Beginners have trouble understanding the relation between defense and preventing opponents from scoring and winning games. You must convince them that defense and preventing a score by opponents is equally as important as scoring points for their own team.

Defense tends to be reactive rather than proactive—a defender will usually react to the moves of an offensive player. Players must learn to be aggressive and initiate action on defense; teach your players to act—not react—when playing defense. With determination and practice a team can develop effective defensive play.

Remember, all team defenses are based on individual fundamental skills. Motivate players to develop pride in their ability to play defense. Any team can be made better by developing a sound team defense.

One of the basic precepts of team defense is to prepare players for action and prevent problems before they arise. For example, a player in quick stance can often anticipate moves by offensive players before they are made and then take that move away. Teach players to be ready for anything, which means being prepared to defend against an opponent's best offensive moves. This makes the defender mentally and physically ready for any other secondary offensive moves by an opponent. Get in a defensive quick stance and stay in that stance.

The main objective of any defense should be to make the other teams do things that they do not want to do. Offense is confidence and rhythm—disrupt that on defense. Take away the opponents' strengths—make them learn how to play differently during games. This means that offenses seldom perform secondary moves and options as well as strengths—it is especially difficult to do this during games. Make them play to their weaknesses by taking away their strengths. Defense is a game of give-and-take; if you take away something, you will likely give up something in return. This applies to strengths/ weaknesses as well as each defensive level and category of defense.

Communication is the glue that holds any team defense together. Effective team defense requires teams to develop and implement excellent communication skills: verbal and nonverbal, talking and listening.

Finally, team defense also will depend on the effectiveness of team offense (ballhandling and taking good shots). Efficient offenses tend to energize and complement team defense as well as take the pressure off of the defense.

DEFENSIVE COURT LEVELS

There are many varieties and styles of defense, and these can be played at different levels of the court (figure 10.1). Coaches can instruct players to begin defending the opposing team at any point on the court.

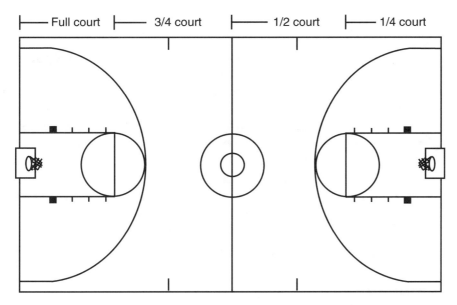

| Full court | 3/4 court | 1/2 court | 1/4 court |

Figure 10.1 Levels of defense—defending team protecting basket on the right.

The full-court team defense is a pressing defense in which defenders guard or pick up opponents as soon as possible all over the court. In a three-quarter-court defense, defenders usually allow the first inbounds pass and then pick up offensive players near the free throw line or the top of the circle. The most common pickup point is at midcourt where the opponents are first guarded at the half-court line. Half-court team defense is the recommended level of defense for most teams through junior high school age. It is also possible to activate team defense at the top of the defensive key. This quarter-court defensive level is used if the other team has greater individual talent.

A team defensive level set at full court or three-quarter court puts more pressure on opponents but forces you to increase court coverage. This level takes away the free movement of opponents in the backcourt but gives the opponent the possible advantage of beating your pressure and getting easy scores from outnumbered situations.

DEFENSIVE CATEGORIES

Team defenses fall into three general categories: player-to-player, in which each defender is assigned to a specific offensive player to guard or defend against; zone, in which each player is assigned a specific area of responsibility depending on the position of the ball and the offensive players; and combination defenses, having elements of both player-to-player and zone defenses.

Player-to-Player Defense

Emphasize the player-to-player defense as the basic defense that all players must master. There are several reasons why the player-to-player defensive approach is valuable. First, the techniques used can be applied in all defenses.

For this reason it should be the primary and probably the only defense used up through the junior high school level of play.

Elementary/middle/junior high school teams often use defenses and pressing tactics to take advantage of the lower skill levels in perimeter shooting and ballhandling. This approach hinders the long-range development of young players and should be discouraged. Players at these age levels should focus on fun and fundamentals with everyone getting the chance to play in every game.

If players in this age group learn the basics of player-to-player defense they will be able to adapt to any defense later. Second, the player-to-player defense is the most challenging and also the most personally rewarding type of defense. No defender can hide in this type of defense: The offense is likely to score an easy basket after any defensive lapse. That is why player-to-player team defense promotes individual responsibility to the team. The basic principles of the defense are explained in chapter 7—Defense.

Zone Defense

Zone defenses assign each player defensive responsibility for a certain area or zone, rather than for an individual offensive player. Zone defenses usually change as the ball moves and are designed to protect a limited area of the court. They are often weaker in the gaps or seams between defenders and on the outside. They can be modified to disguise those weaknesses.

Zone defenses can be designed to give and take away also; sagging zones give up more outside shots but take away the inside. Lane or pressure zones may take away outside shots but they may be vulnerable inside.

Zones can also be changed to lane defenses designed to intercept passes, trapping defenses (two players double-teaming one offensive player with the ball), or sagging defenses where the inside area near the basket is heavily protected.

The 2-3 Zone.   The most commonly used zone defense is the 2-3 zone. Figure 10.2a shows the basic coverage areas and figure 10.2b the weak areas of this defense. Use this defense when playing a team with a good post player or when you need to ensure good corner coverage.

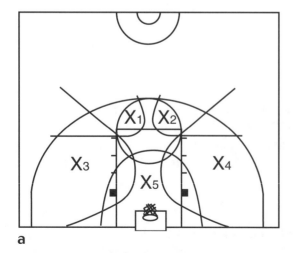 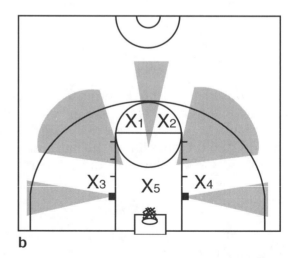

Figure 10.2a–b   The 2-3 zone defense: (a) coverage and (b) weakness areas.

Figures 10.3a and 10.3.b show the player shifts with the ball in different positions.

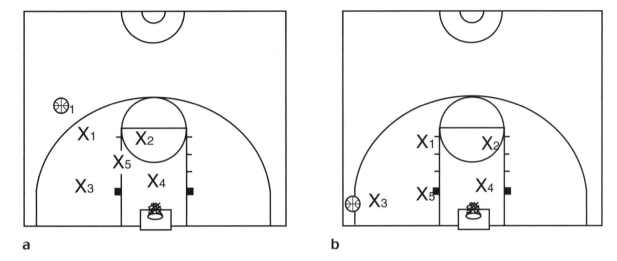

Figure 10.3a–b The 2-3 zone *(a)* with ball on the wing and *(b)* with ball in the frontcourt corner.

The 1-3-1 Zone. The 1-3-1 zone defense is also commonly used to cover the high post and wing area well. It is strong in the center, wings, and point. The coverage and gaps are shown in figures 10.4a and 10.4b. The shifts of the 1-3-1 zone are shown in figures 10.5a and 10.5b with the ball in the corner and on the wing, respectively. Note that most zones revert to a 2-3 formation with the ball in the corner.

The 1-2-2 Zone. The 1-2-2 zone defense has good coverage on the perimeter but is vulnerable inside. Its coverage and weakness areas are depicted in figures 10.6a and b. The movement and shifts of this 1-2-2 zone (figures 10.7a and b) are similar to the 1-3-1 zone shown earlier.

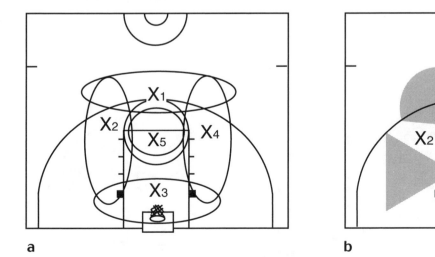

Figure 10.4a–b The 1-3-1 zone defense: *(a)* coverage, and *(b)* weakness areas.

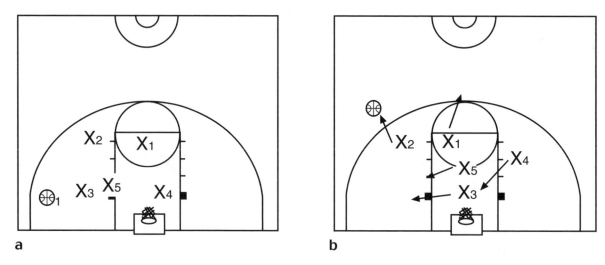

Figure 10.5a–b The 1-3-1 zone *(a)* with ball in the corner and *(b)* with ball on the wing.

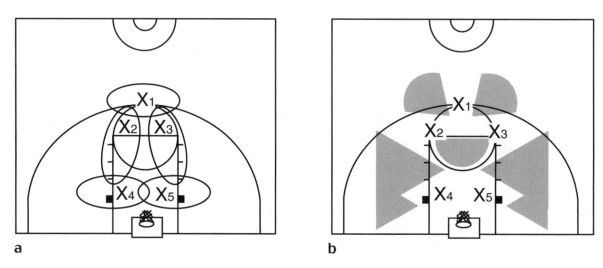

Figure 10.6a–b The 1-2-2 zone defense: *(a)* coverage and *(b)* weakness areas.

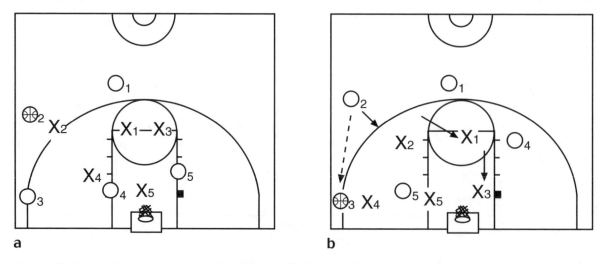

Figure 10.7a–b The 1-2-2 zone defense: *(a)* ball on wing, *(b)* ball in corner.

Combination Defense

Combination defenses may take several forms. Generally, they are used to take away an opponent's strength and confuse offenses. For example, a triangle-and-two defense might be used against a team with only two good scorers; a box-and-one could be used against an opponent with one high scoring or key player.

Triangle-and-Two. Two defenders are assigned player-to-player on selected opponents while three defenders play a triangular zone as shown in figure 10.8. To use this defense effectively, coaches must decide on the extent of floor coverage and shifts for the triangle zone defenders and how they want the two player-to-player defenders to play (tight, loose, ball denial, etc.). This defense takes away the effectiveness of two offensive players (usually perimeter) but is vulnerable in other outside shooting areas.

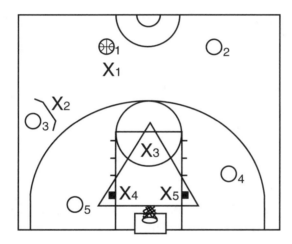

Figure 10.8 The triangle-and-two combination defense (X_1 and X_2 player-to-player).

Box- or Diamond-and-One. One defender is player-to-player while the other four play a zone defense near the basket. This works well against a team with one outstanding scorer or ballhandler. Two forms of this defense are shown in figures 10.9a and 10.9b. Assign the opposing player who is the best scorer, ballhandler, or team leader to the best player-to-player defender. Determine who is the key player for the other team and how to take away that player's strength.

This defense takes away the effectiveness of one player with four zone players being used to help and protect the basket, but it can also be vulnerable to outside shooting.

Pressing Defenses

Player-to-player pressure defenses can be played at any level: half court, three-quarter court, or full court. All basic principles apply, but helping situations are much more challenging as defense expands to full court. A premium is placed on individual defenders stopping and pressuring the ballhandler because of the greater floor area to cover. This type of pressure defense was first developed in the 1940s in men's college basketball.

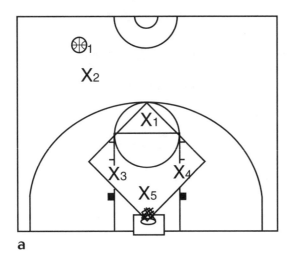 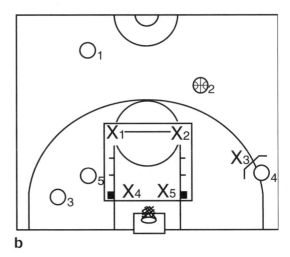

Figure 10.9a–b *(a)* The diamond-and-one combination defense. *(b)* The box-and-one combination defense.

Zone pressure defenses can be played at all levels. Probably the most famous instance of a full-court zone press was popularized in the unprecedented success experienced at UCLA under John Wooden. The staple of his first national collegiate championship team was the full-court 2-2-1 zone press, as seen in figure 10.10. Zone presses tend to speed up game tempo, while player-to-player pressure defenses may slow tempo.

This press usually is used as a containing press, keeping the ball out of the middle, that usually will set at least one sideline trap before half court (figure 10.11). Note that X_1 covers the middle, X_5 the sideline, and X_3 protects the basket.

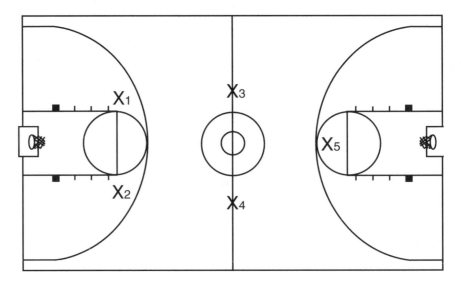

Figure 10.10 2-2-1 zone press.

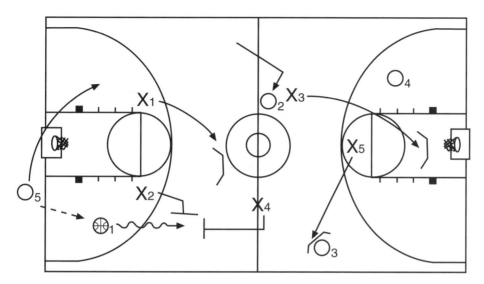

Figure 10.11 2-2-1 zone trap.

Decisions need to be made about when to trap (usually when the dribble comes to the defense and before the half-court line), how to rotate, when to drop back to the regular half-court defense, and the type of defense to transition into on the half court. If player-to-player defense is selected, one method would be to retreat to the basic defense after one trap: protect the basket, stop the ball, and pick up all open players (in that order). Communication is a key in that transition.

A half-court zone press is exemplified by the 1-3-1 defense used by the Kentucky team coached by Joe B. Hall that won a national championship in 1978. The basic set is shown as an extended 1-3-1, seen in figure 10.12.

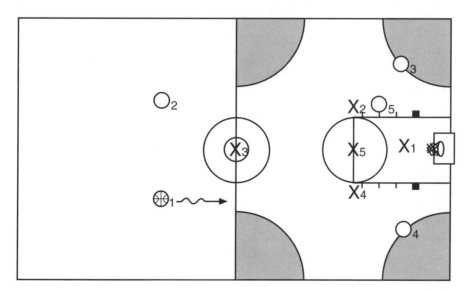

Figure 10.12 1-3-1 half-court zone press.

The perimeter players X$_3$, X$_4$, and X$_2$ play in the passing lanes and force the offense to pass over the top (slower passes). The ball is forced into the corners and trapped, as shown in figure 10.13.

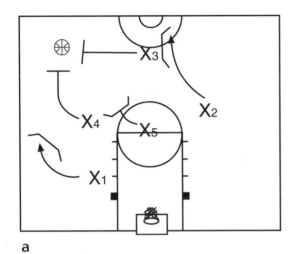

a

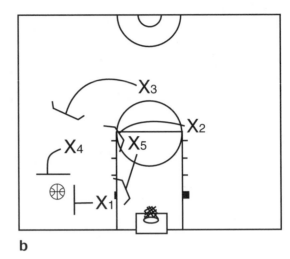

b

Figure 10.13a–b Corner traps. *(a)* Near halfcourt, *(b)* near baseline.

Coaching Points for Team Defense

- Select one defense as the primary team defense. The player-to-player defense is recommended up through junior high school level.
- Make attitude and motivation major concerns when developing team defensive play.
- Focus on practicing against all offenses. Prevent surprises for the defense during games by fully preparing your team for all situations in practice.
- There should be equal emphasis on offense and defense, but more time should be spent on offense (requires ballhandling and shooting).
- All defenses require defenders to play hard—all five players must move with every pass or dribble.
- Team defense begins with an effective transition from offense to defense.
- Team defense ends with the defensive rebound, steal, or opponent's turnover.
- Effective defense requires communication: verbal and nonverbal, talking and listening.

Team Defense Checklist

☐ General principles developed
☐ Defensive fundamental skills
☐ Stance and steps
☐ Defense on the ball (live ball/dribble)
☐ Defense off the ball (closed/open)
☐ Defense closeouts (off ball to on ball)
☐ On ball to off ball
☐ Defense special situations

___ post defense
___ help and decide (bluff/switch/trap)
___ on-ball screens
___ off-ball screens
___ double screens

___ defensive charge
___ pressure the shot
___ loose ball

☐ Defensive rebounding
☐ Team defense
☐ Player to player
☐ Zone
☐ Combination
☐ Levels of defense
☐ Zone press
☐ Out-of-bounds, under
☐ Out-of-bounds, side
☐ Defensive free throws

TEAM DEFENSE DRILLS

Defense needs to be learned for all situations and built up from individual play (one-on-one) progressively to team play (five-on-five). Please refer to the individual defensive drills in chapter 7 (Defense, Page 119) as the foundation for developing team defense.

- moving stance and steps
- line drill—individual defense
- closeouts—one-on-one, two-on-two, three-on-three, four-on-four
- on ball-off ball two-on-two
- defensive slide—moving stance and steps

Half-Court–Three-on-Three, Four-on-Four (Shell Drill)

PURPOSE

Break down all two-person, three-person offensive play situations and learn to defend them in a team situation.

EQUIPMENT

Ball, half court, and 8 to 12 players.

PROCEDURE

Each practice can emphasize a selected offensive situation to defend. Prepare the team for all situations (no game surprises). Set up a drill rotation; offense to defense to off-court.

OPTIONS

- on-ball screens
- off-ball screens
- double screens
- use of traps
- two out, two in (perimeter, post)
- four outside players, flash post on the cut
- give-and-go moves
- dribble penetration focus
- post play (single, double)
- three out, one in
- three in, one out
- one-guard front or two-guard front

Half-Court to Full-Court Drills—Three-on-Three, Four-on-Four, Five-on-Five

PURPOSE

Practice basic half-court defense and transition to offense; practice basic half-court offense and transition to defense.

EQUIPMENT

Ball, full court, and at least two groups of players.

PROCEDURE

Set up selected offensive situations to defend and then transition to offense on missed shots; work on selected offensive situations and then carry out an effective defensive transition on made or missed baskets.

OPTIONS

- three-on-three
- four-on-four
- five-on-five team offense and defense

Full-Court Drills—Three-on-Three, Five-on-Five

PURPOSE

Teach all phases of defense progressively; three-on-three breakdowns and five-on-five with full teams.

EQUIPMENT

Ball and full court with at least two groups of players.

PROCEDURE

For three-on-three full court, it is recommended that players/groups change after no more than three circuits of full court up and back. The ball must be dribbled over half court, and no breakaway lob passes are allowed in an early progression.

Appendix: Practice Planning

One strongly recommended tip for organization is developing a *written* practice plan for *every* practice. Be as efficient as possible in the limited time available for practices. Some basic principles for developing a practice plan are

- develop a drill package that fits your system, to include all phases of the game;
- offensive—fast break, shooting, fundamentals (line drills), post and perimeter, rebounding, team;
- defense—transition, fundamentals, on ball, off ball, off to on ball, on to off ball, screens, traps, rebounding, team;
- devote 60 percent of practice time to offense, 40 percent to defense (equal emphasis);
- practice fundamentals at each practice;
- include field goal shooting and free throw shooting at each practice;
- practice all offensive and defensive situations—game simulation;
- alternate hard and easy drills;
- use variety and short drill segments: three minutes, five minutes, seven minutes, eight minutes;
- have an emphasis/theme for the day;
- explain one basketball rule per day;
- teach new concepts earlier in practice;
- stretch after practice as you evaluate, give feedback, and motivate;
- schedule enjoyment or fun drills; insert one each workout;
- meet or make notes right after practice to evaluate or preplan for next practice;
- use a practice plan form; team division, announcements, equipment, time-drill-teaching notes, evaluation and diagram sections;
- be able to demonstrate and explain all fundamental skills; and
- use a "one minute assessment" with players and coaches to provide status and progress measures and promote learning. This assessment is done by identifying one skill or drill that was done well (correctly) and why you though it was done well and by identifying one area of improvement and how that area can be improved. For example, you could tell a player, "Your shot is improving because your balance is better (no sideways drift), but you could improve your shot more with better follow-through (always lock your elbow). Finish on positive note.

SAMPLE PRACTICE PLAN

Teams:

Date: _____ 10-18 _____

Practice #: ___3___

Black		Gold		White	
Dean	1	Mel	1	Andy	1
Rod	2	Pete	2	Dave	2
Jay	3	Roy	3	Tim	3
Ron	4	John	4	Jerry	4
Paul	5	Tony	5	Bo	5

Announce Theme Rule:	Be quick but don't hurry, 5 second count.	Equipment Needed: 15 balls, tossbacks

Time	Drill	Critical Cue
3:20–3:25	Meet	Theme/rule
3:25–3:35	Line Drill	O zag/Live ball moves/2 on 1 feed pass and closeout
3:35–3:40	2 on 0, fast break	Split the floor
3:40–3:48	3 on 0, 2FB	Top speed under control/middle dribble only
3:48–3:53	Stance Reaction	Get low and stay low
3:53–4:03	1 on 1 O - D	React to ball/2 dribble max on O
4:03–4:08	Spin Pass FG	30 sec sets/feet ready—hands ready
4:08–4:23	Breakdown	Inside—Mikan/Figure 8 reb/post moves Outside—dribble moves—pace/c-o/h-s/spin/pullback
4:23–4:28	Closeout	1 on 1 (shot only/baseline drive)
4:28–4:31	Water/FT	Row 2 and water break
4:31–4:39	Closeout Rebound	3 on 3—communicate/make contact
4:39–4:44	Catch and Face	Wing position—dribble drive (layup/J)
4:44–4:59	Motion O—5 on 0	Skeleton—spacing/pass and move (cut/screen)/TT
4:59–5:14	FB - 5 on 0	Made and missed—D to O transition/O to D transition
5:14–5:25	FB—5 on 2,3	Blitz FB live—read the defense
5:25–5:30	Stretch and Meet	Evaluate/Positive Note/Next day

Notes/Evaluation:

Drill Finder

About the Authors

Jerry V. Krause has been coaching the basics of basketball since 1959. His experience at the elementary, high school, college, and Olympic levels uniquely qualifies him to write a book that helps to improve the skills of players at all levels of play.

Krause is a professor of sport philosophy and the director of instruction for West Point U.S. Military Academy's Department of Physical Education. He received the 1988 State Honor Award from the Washington Alliance for Health, Physical Education, Recreation and Dance for outstanding teaching and coaching in college physical education.

A member of the National Association of Basketball Coaches (NABC), Krause is the chair of their National Research Committee and wrote the 1986 Code of Ethics. Krause received the 1998 NABC Appreciation Award for lifetime contributions to basketball. He is also a member and past president of the National Association of Intercollegiate Athletics (NAIA) Basketball Coaches Association.

Krause is also the author of the popular, *The Basketball Bible* and the *Basketball Resource Guide*, as well as nine other basketball coaching books and 18 basketball teaching videos.

Don Meyer has reached unprecedented heights in his first 23 seasons as head men's basketball coach at Lipscomb University in Nashville, Tennessee. He reached the 600-win plateau faster than any other coach in college basketball history. Named the National Coach of the Year in 1989 and 1990, Meyer was inducted to the NAIA Hall of Fame in 1993. He resides in Nashville.

Jerry Meyer, Don's son, has begun his coaching career as an assistant coach at Vanderbilt University. After a prolific Tennessee high school career that included consecutive Mr. AA Basketball awards, he set assist records in college at Lipscomb and the University of Minnesota, Duluth. He was named both All-American and Academic All-American during his college career. He currently lives in Nashville.

Advanced Skill Development
Basketball Skills and Drills II

Video 1 - **Basketball and Body Control**
- ➢ stance
- ➢ steps
- ➢ pass and catch
- ➢ live ball moves

- ➢ starts and stops
- ➢ turns and jumps
- ➢ dribbling
- ➢ screens

Video 2 - **Basketball Scoring**
- ➢ layups
- ➢ post shots

- ➢ set/jump shots
- ➢ free throws

Video 3 - **Basketball Defense and Rebounding**
- ➢ on the ball
- ➢ off to on the ball
- ➢ O rebounding

- ➢ off the ball
- ➢ on to off the ball
- ➢ D rebounding

Video 4 - **Basketball Drills for Skills**
- ➢ perimeter and post play
- ➢ individual and small group development

- ➢ player workouts

The skills foundation for __any__ player and __any__ system.

Please copy order form below

- -

Please RUSH the following items:

- ❑ Video 1 -Basketball and Body Control $35
- ❑ Video 2 -Basketball Scoring $35
- ❑ Video 3 -Basketball Defense and Rebounding $35
- ❑ Video 4 -Basketball Drills for Skills $35
- ❑ Set of All Four Videos (save $40) $100
- ❑ *Skills and Drills* CD-ROM $20

Name _____

School _____

Address _____

City_____

State _____ Zip _____

Return order to: Don Meyer
Bison Basketball Office
David Lipscomb University
Nashville, TN 37204-3951

Sorry, no credit cards or phone orders.

Make checks payable to:
Don Meyer Enterprises, Inc.

2335

Also available (videos @ $20 each):

from
Basic Skill Development
Basketball Skills and Drills I

- ❑ Field Goal Shooting
  (set/jump shots)
- ❑ Field Goal Shooting
  (layup/3-point)
- ❑ Free Throw Shooting
- ❑ Footwork
- ❑ Pass and Catch
- ❑ Dribbling
- ❑ Teaching Tips
- ❑ Get Open to Score
- ❑ Perimeter Play
- ❑ Post Play
- ❑ Setting and Using
- ❑ Screens
- ❑ Individual Defense
- ❑ Rebounding
- ❑ Team Attitude
- ❑ Full Set of 14 Videos (save $80) $200
- ❑ Player Video Package of 7 (save $40) $100
  - • Field Goal Shooting (both)
  - • Free Throw Shooting
  - • Footwork
  - • Pass and Catch
  - • Dribbling
  - • Rebounding

Add $5 for Shipping and Handling.

Total Order: $_____

For more information please call:
(615) 269-1822 or 800-333-4358

Books to boost basketball
skills, conditioning, and performance

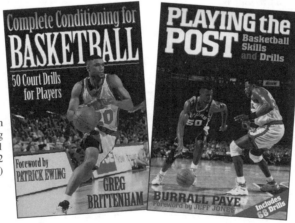

Morgan Wootten
Foreword by John Wooden
Item PWOO0446
ISBN 0-88011-446-0
$19.95 ($29.95 Canadian)

National Basketball Conditioning
Coaches Association (NBCCA)
Foreword by Lenny Wilkens,
Head Coach, Atlanta Hawks
Item PNBC0687
ISBN 0-88011-687-0
$17.95 ($24.95 Canadian)

This book covers every facet of building a successful
basketball program and team. Morgan Wootten shows the
teaching and motivation techniques, game strategies, and
winning formula he's used to build and maintain the
dynasty at DeMatha. Wootten is considered by many to
be the best basketball coach of all time.

Ten of the top NBA strength and conditioning coaches
combined to create this manual designed specifically
to improve basketball performance. A higher vertical
jump can lead to more rebounds; greater quickness
and flexibility will help you play tougher D. Take it
from the experts and take your conditioning program
and competitive performance to the highest level.

Greg Brittenham
Foreword by Patrick Ewing
Item PBRI0881
ISBN 0-87322-881-2
$15.95 ($23.95 Canadian)

Burrall Paye
Foreword by Jeff Jones
Item PPAY0979
ISBN 0-87322-979-7
$15.95 ($22.95 Canadian)

New York Knicks' strength and conditioning coach
Greg Brittenham shares the exercises, drills, and
training programs he's found most effective for
basketball players. This book shows how to develop
players' athletic abilities—speed, power, endurance,
agility, coordination, balance, and reaction time—while
at the same time working on sport-specific skills.

While the 3-point shot may be popular, games are
still won and lost in and around the free-throw lane.
Players will become more effective in the paint with
the superb teaching of skills and wide selection of
drills in *Playing the Post*. This book will help you
develop the inside moves to score three points the
old-fashioned way—powering to the hoop for the
score and converting the free throw.